LIBRARY
OKALOOSA-WALTON JUNIOR COLLEGE

D0991321

THE GLORY
THAT WAS
GRUB STREET

THE GLORY THAT WAS GRUB STREET

Impressions of Contemporary Authors

BY

ARTHUR ST. JOHN ADCOCK

WITH THIRTY-TWO CAMERA STUDIES
BY
E. O. HOPPÉ

Essay Index Reprint Series

BOOKS FOR LIBRARIES PRESS
FREEPORT, NEW YORK

PR
471
A32
1969

First Published 1928
Reprinted 1969

STANDARD BOOK NUMBER:
8369-1388-4

LIBRARY OF CONGRESS CATALOG CARD NUMBER:
72-99678

PRINTED IN THE UNITED STATES OF AMERICA

LIBRARY
OKALOOSA-WALTON JUNIOR COLLEGE

PREFACE

THE title of this second volume of "The Gods of Modern Grub Street" was originally given to it for the comfort of my publishers and would have been altered if, before going to press, I could have thought of a better one. It is not intended to suggest that every author once lived in Grub Street, nor that those who did were not glad to get out; it is intended to suggest that the Grub Street tradition has grown and put forth branches until it is no longer a mere street but a whole literary world of many-coloured romance which seems to be as fascinating to the artistic temperament as webs are to flies, so that one may almost say of it, as Chaucer said of the married state, that

> "They who are in would fain get out,
> And they who are out would fain get in."

Anyhow, you find the author who formerly dwelt in Grub Street, but has become prosperous and changed his address, will confess that, looking back from the affluence and tame security of the present, he realises that when he lived in the Street, and everything seemed possible and nothing sure, those

v

75148

PREFACE

early days were more stimulating, richer in excitement, adventure, even in happiness, than he was aware of at the time, and he has wistful feelings that if he could return there something of the freedom and enthusiasm he lost with his youth might be restored to him. On the other hand, authors who fortunately (or unfortunately) had no initial difficulties to overcome but walked or were handsomely carried to success along paths strewn with roses and other soft things, have unsettling suspicions that they have missed something and often take to Bohemian haunts and habits under the impression that they are thus breaking "their birth's invidious bar" and doing the thing properly; and of course they are, if they sufficiently think they are. So, in a sense, you may say that all authors belong to Grub Street, and the glory that was Grub Street belongs to all authors, so long as they have left the place behind them or never lodged in it. Which applies no less to American than to English authors. When the Pilgrim Fathers emigrated they evidently took their share of the Grub Street tradition with them and planted it in that soil, and, from information received, it is flourishing there sturdily.

No criticism of one's contemporaries can, I suppose, be final, especially where they have not yet finished their work (Mary Webb, for example, is much more highly esteemed now than when she

PREFACE

was alive); therefore I have, I hope with seemly diffidence, left that part of the business largely to posterity. I have freely expressed some impressions and opinions, simply because I happened to have them, and a man is entitled to do what he likes with his own; but, in the main, my aim has been to introduce certain authors to the reader by means of presenting, so far as I could, their personalities and careers and so helping him, perhaps, to a closer understanding of the books that are more or less a revelation of those careers and those personalities.

I should like to explain why one article here is unaccompanied by a portrait. Mr. Robert Hichens lives much abroad, and my friend, Mr. E. O. Hoppé, whose sensitive artistry is responsible for all the portraits in this book, was unable to secure the necessary sitting. There is no need, I feel, to apologise for this omission, since it has given opportunity to gratify many readers by including, at the end of the article in which reference is made to him, a portrait of Mr. Sinclair Lewis, nowadays the most popular American author among us; who has, otherwise, been reserved for the third volume.

My thanks are due to Mrs. Nancy Sheppard (sister-in-law of Mr. Alfred Tresidder Sheppard) for the drawing of myself on the wrapper of this book.

St. J. A.

CONTENTS

CONTENTS

x

THE GLORY
THAT WAS
GRUB STREET

GEORGE BERNARD SHAW

IF the law of cause and effect were in proper working order, George Bernard Shaw would, I suppose, be much more disliked than most of us are, for he goes about, and has always gone about, saying and doing continually the sort of things that make enemies. All his life he has been at war with our social, political and general orthodoxies; when these happen to amuse him he is not discreet enough to pretend to take them seriously, and his laughter naturally irritates the many who take them very seriously indeed and are quite unable to see the funny side of their solemnity or to believe they are capable of anything that could lay them open to ridicule. They may go to church on Sunday and join audibly in the confession that like sheep they have gone astray, that they are miserable sinners and have no health in them, and make no attempt, before next Sunday, to alter their manner of living, yet resent the ribald suggestion that their conduct and philosophy of life are in any way laughable. Shaw has been mistaken for an incorrigible jester because, instead

1

of losing his temper and furiously denouncing the follies and hypocrisies of mankind, or going after the foolish with a whip (though he has done that on occasion), he is more inclined to laugh at them; he finds a subject for farce or comedy where the conventional reformer would find a text for a sermon. And, whatever can be said against them, it is some justification for his methods that while other sermons have emptied the churches, his have filled the theatres.

I have said he has been mistaken for a jester; but worse than that has been said of him. He has been scornfully described by important and other persons as a mountebank, a poseur, a cheapjack bent on blatantly advertising himself and his wares; average men and women in all circles of society have found it impossible to feel that he is in earnest about anything, has any convictions, any consistent doctrine, is not merely a clever buffoon, ready to say whatever would tickle the groundlings and provoke a guffaw; is not altogether shallow, flippant, irreverent, wholly insincere; and for this he has largely himself to blame. My own conviction is, though it was not always, that there is no sincerer man among his contemporaries, none more sensitively humane, more religiously in earnest. He knew his own mind from the first; he had his own common-sense gospel of social honesty, justice, righteousness, and was preaching it in the press, from the platform and the stage before he had much of a hearing, and has gone on preaching it ever since. But his invincible common-sense told him he could do no effective preaching nor hope to sell even what was worth buying until he had secured an audience, and, laying himself open to the charge of being a quack and a charlatan, he deliberately adopted the practices of the mountebank to attract a crowd and to make it listen to him after it was collected.

"Really," he says in the preface to "Major Barbara," "the English do not deserve to have great men. They allowed Butler to die practically unknown, whilst I, a comparatively insignificant Irish journalist, was leading them by the nose into an advertisement of me which has made my own life a burden. . . . It cannot be denied that the English are only too anxious to recognise a man of genius if somebody will kindly point him out to them. Having pointed myself out in this manner with some success, I now point out Samuel Butler. . . . There are living men whose originality and power are as obvious as Butler's; and when they die that fact will be discovered. Meanwhile I recommend them to insist on their own merits as an important part of their own business." He had resolutely done this himself, and eight years before he wrote

3

that preface to "Major Barbara" said in the article which closed his connection with the *Saturday Review*, that for ten years "with an unprecedented pertinacity and obstinacy I have been dinning into the public head that I am an extraordinarily witty, brilliant and clever man. That is now part of the public opinion of England; and no power in heaven or earth will ever change it." Though this happens to be true, such blatant assertion of it might be taken as evidence of a colossal self-conceit, but Shaw is too sensible a man with too keen a sense of humour to be conceited. He was probably conscious of his own genius, as Shakespeare was when he wrote

> "Not marble nor the gilded monuments
> Of princes shall outlive this powerful rhyme,"

but when he blew a trumpet about it, when he disparaged Shakespeare and acclaimed himself as the greater dramatist, he was not actuated by vanity, but by a sound business instinct; since the world accepts a man at his valuation of himself, as a penniless author fighting for recognition and a livelihood, Shaw threw modesty to the dogs and instead of blushing unseen and wasting his sweetness on the desert air, accommodated himself to the world's stupidity. "In order to gain a hearing," he has written, "it was necessary for

4

me to attain the footing of a privileged lunatic with the licence of a jester. My method has therefore been to take the utmost trouble to find the right thing to say and then to say it with the utmost levity. And all the time the real joke is that I am in earnest." Even if he never really considered Shakespeare his inferior, he was jesting in earnest when he said that he did—he knew that such a literary blasphemy would rouse hundreds by whom he would otherwise have been neglected to talk of him, write of him, rage against him and so advertise him into a profitable notoriety, and that is why he said it. Those who, still blind to his greatness, say he is an impudent zany whose boastful blether and bewildering antics have hypnotised and bamboozled the public, are only confirming his estimate of that public and vindicating the ways of Shaw to man.

The first time I ever set eyes on him was many years ago when he was a young man and I was younger. It was in a hall not far from Swiss Cottage station, and he was there to deliver an address on the , middle classes. The hall was packed with obviously middle-class people, and he told them in the most genial but devastating manner all sorts of facts about themselves—about their snobbishness, their petty conventionalities, their false gentilities, the plodding subservience with which they bore all the burdens it was customary for politicians to impose on them—and the hall roared with laughter and enjoyed every word of it. If he had said the same things angrily, fiercely, with a scorn that was veiled in no humour, no flippancies, he would have stung that audience to resentment; if it had not interrupted and shouted him down, it would have gone home boiling with wrath, too roused and insulted to do anything but blindly refute his indictments and justify itself. Not a few might, by way of protest, have marched out and left half the lecture unheard. As it was, they all stayed to the finish, and would have stayed longer if he had gone on. They cheered him enthusiastically when he sat down, and departed in the best of tempers. But they had got some hard truths; the pill was sugarcoated, but it was an undoubtable pill; and when they repeated Shaw's jests to each other afterwards and laughed again at his wit, the intelligent among them must have been conscious that what he said was true as well as whimsical, and it would bear the more fruit because it fell upon their minds like a pleasant and enlivening dew and not like a destroying thunder-storm.

That is Shaw's way; and in his plays he has not departed from it. I am old enough to remember when they were usually produced at select little theatres that were filled with select, devout worshippers, with cranks, faddists, earnest admirers, and a remnant who came because a taste for Shaw had come to be regarded as a sign of intellectual superiority, just as others go to church because it is considered a religious thing to do so. But he has grown out of those swaddling bands into a full and robust life until, nowadays, the same plays and those he has written since are put on at any of our largest theatres as popular entertainments. You may see parsons, politicians, military men, business men, plebeians in the gallery and aristocrats in boxes and stalls listening to "Arms and the Man," "John Bull and his Other Island," "Man and Superman," "Major Barbara," "The Showing-up of Blanco Posnet," "Androcles and the Lion," "Pygmalion," "Heartbreak House," "Back to Methusaleh," "Saint Joan," obviously enjoying the wit, the sly irony, the unorthodox teaching and humane, common-sense philosophy of them, even when these are levelled at their own beliefs and practises and satirise the opinions they hold and the lives they live. Like that audience at Swiss Cottage, they take their medicine gladly because the brilliance of his wit and the humour which clothes the sincerity of his hatred of wrong and cant and cruelty and humbug make it palatable. And you may depend that a physic so taken, since

7

it is taken, is at least as efficacious as that which
is so raw and offensive to the palate that none will
go willingly to the place where it is to be given to
them. I was assured darkly, the other day, by
a famous specialist, "I ought not to say so, but
there is a lot of truth in Shaw's 'Doctor's Dilemma'."
The significance of the admission lay in the fact
that he was deprecating the operation another
specialist had recommended.

I doubt whether any man has attacked more
social evils and respectable shibboleths, or had a
profounder, more far-reaching influence on his
own time; yet, however it may have been before
he had lived long enough for the world to know
him so well, he has fewer enemies now than have
most public men who, not having a tithe of his
outspokenness, have never told any truths that
were unpleasant to their own supporters. Indeed,
I question whether he has many real enemies nowadays at all. So when a prominent politician
recently referred to him as "a brilliant clown" I
felt this would comfort Shaw and help to reassure
him; it would indicate to him that he was still
hitting the mark, for, of course, considering the
amount and variety of public opinion he has been
and is up against, he ought to have a multitude
of enemies, and if he were not in himself so unfail-
ingly good-humoured, so genial and ready to take

and respond to the worst a foe can give him, he would. If he never turns the other cheek, he never expects the other man to do so, and rather hopes that he won't. He loves a fight, and joys in receiving and giving hard knocks; but, unlike the reformer Hood scarifies, he does not want to give anyone two black eyes for being blind; he is merely anxious to knock some vision into him. He remains so unassuming and charming a personality that, talking with him, it is difficult to realise that he began by boasting himself into fame, that he has come through so many scrimmages and is perhaps the most aggressive, opinionated man alive and the most uncompromising. The legend that he is egotistical and (except for strictly business purposes) a braggart may seem more than legendary to some, but I am pretty sure he could not if he tried robe himself in the pomposities, the dignified aloofness of bearing that many of the great wear, or have worn, unblamed. Unlike Tennyson, Carlyle, and other of the famous dead and living, he does not dress like a stage brigand or sit in a shrine to be adored; if any man of his eminence is less pretentious in manner or appearance, more easily and naturally gracious and sociable, I have never met him.

I have written nothing of formal biography, and there is no need of much. Shaw tells us in the preface to "John Bull's Other Island" "When I say that I am an Irishman, I mean that I was born in Ireland, and that my native language is the English of Swift, and not the unspeakable jargon of the mid-nineteenth century newspapers. My extraction is the extraction of most Englishmen: that is, I have no trace in me of the commercially imported North Spanish strain which passes for aboriginal Irish: I am a genuine Irishman of the Danish, Norman, Cromwellian, and (of course) Scotch invasions. I am violently and arrogantly Protestant by family tradition; but let no English Government therefore count on my allegiance: I am English enough to be an inveterate Republican and Home Ruler. It is true that one of my grandfathers was an Orangeman; but then his sister was an abbess; and his uncle, I am proud to say, was hanged as a rebel." His father was easy-going, attractive, impecunious, and is said to have been proud of his kinship to a baronet; his mother was a beautiful Irish opera singer, and from her he inherits the passion for music which discounts the assertion often made that he has no poetry in his composition. He came to London in 1876, when he was twenty; and if his early struggles convinced him that "our first duty—a duty to which every other consideration should be sacrificed—is not to be poor," and hardened him, from a sense of that duty, to embark on his campaign of self-advertisement, it did not steel him against sympathy with young authors who are going through the purgatory he has left behind him, and his practical kindnesses to such would destroy his reputation as a cynic if they were all revealed. He began by writing four novels which were clever but not successful; one, I believe, remained for long unpublished. He joined the Fabian Society, and wrote tracts on Socialism, assiduously joined in socialistic debates and practised the art of public speaking; became a vestryman of St. Pancras, and agitated the dull waters of parochial politics; and before he established himself as a playwright he had served a longish term as music critic on the *Star* and the *World*, and dramatic critic on the *Saturday Review*. He started on the *Star* as a leader-writer, but, I have heard T. P. say, as he could not keep socialism out of his leaders and the *Star* was an organ of Liberalism, he was, for safety, turned on to music, and one of the most brilliant of music and dramatic critics was lost when he gave himself over to writing plays for others to criticise.

As for the manner of man who has emerged from this tempestuous career, and who, from passing as an insincere farceur, has, especially since the appearance of "Back to Methusaleh" and "Saint Joan," come to be regarded as a prophet, the best book that has been written on him is "George Bernard Shaw", by G. K. Chesterton, and I should like to quote from that a noble judgment to which the majority are, at length, beginning to subscribe:

"Anyone who knows Shaw's work," writes G. K. C., "will recognise in it Shaw himself. There exists by accident an early and beardless portrait of him which fully suggests in the severity and purity of its lines some of the early ascetic portraits of the beardless Christ. However he may shout profanities or seek to shatter the shrines, there is always something about him which suggests that in a sweeter and more solid civilisation he would have been a great saint. He would have been a saint of a sternly ascetic, perhaps of a sternly negative type. But he has this strange note of the saint in him: that he is literally unworldly. Worldliness has no human magic for him; he is not bewitched by rank nor drawn on by conviviality at all. He could not understand the intellectual surrender of the snob. He is perhaps a defective character; but he is not a mixed one. All the virtues he has are heroic virtues. Shaw is like the Venus of Milo; all there is of him is admirable."

THOMAS BURKE.

THOMAS BURKE

IT used to be a canon of criticism, not so long ago, that all great art is impersonal. We were told (when I was young one distinguished critic told me in most reverent and emphatic terms) that Shakespeare could not be found in his plays or poems; that these were the sublime creations of his intellect and imagination, and that he had kept himself out of them with the perfect reticence of the supreme artist. It was a generally accepted faith. When somebody said that with his sonnets Shakespeare had unlocked his heart, wasn't it Browning who exclaimed, "then so much the less Shakespeare he!"

But this notion that the artist writes in a spirit of serene detachment from his work is only one of the many critical theories we try on from time to time and quietly discard as soon as we find they won't fit. The fact is that every author, especially the novelist, is consciously or unconsciously autobiographical. His personal experiences are naturally, almost inevitably, the raw material with which he makes his stories and his characters. He may not use such experiences literally; he adapts them, adds to them, varies or amplifies them with imaginary details; he joins up incidents that, when they happened to him, had no connection with each other; in the same way, he creates a character by blending in one man or woman the characters of two or three different men or women he has known. The facts about himself are in his books, some disguised closely, some very slightly, and some not disguised at all.

Perhaps no contemporary is more autobiographical than Thomas Burke. You may not always be able to disentangle it and feel sure of where truth ends and fiction comes in to leaven it, but much of his own life-story runs through his "Nights in Town", through that most personal and poignant of his novels, "The Wind and the Rain", and you have glimpses of it in his recent volume of "Essays", and here and there in many other of his sketches and stories. When the boy who is telling his tale in "The Wind and the Rain" tells how the reading of a popular semi-literary weekly first woke a love of literature in him, how he began to borrow books from the Public Library, occasionally straining his scanty salary to buy them and, groping his way to the poetry and prose that most appealed to him, found a way of escape out of the poverty and drabness of his surroundings—this is not fiction but Burke going back in remembrance over the road he has travelled himself:

"London was now touched with a new magic—the magic of noble association; and though I couldn't travel with Ariel I could feel the brush of his wings. The hard lines of Poultry became softened because Hood had been born there, and Waterloo Bridge was charged with passion and terror. Oxford Street was no more a busy main street; it was steeped in darkling clouds, not of London, but of bizarre countries of the fancy; and at every corner fluttered the imperial purple of the opium eater. (Him I could understand and I carried him about with me for weeks.) The horrid terra-cotta of the Prudential Building assumed grace as covering the site of Chatterton's last lodging. Tower Hill was lit with Otway, Bankside with Shakespeare and Greene, and the Borough High Street with the Canterbury Pilgrims. Even my own court, Bussell's Grove, took something of the spell. I dramatised it. Perhaps Chatterton or Savage had lived in just such a place as this."

It is Burke again putting his own memories into the narrative when it goes on to picture the boy's bitter sense of the social and other disadvantages against which he had to make headway; his hopelessness of ever being able to emancipate himself from the ill-paid drudgery of office-life; what it was that gave him his first idea for a story; how he wrote it, then "punched it out slowly on the office typewriter" after the staff was gone, and sent it to *T.P.'s Weekly*. It came back, but half a dozen words on the rejection slip encouraged him to go

on writing; and the record of his many failures
and few successes in the years when he was between
seventeen and twenty is true not only of Burke but
of all young authors who were

> "born
> Under the starving sign of Capricorn"

and have had to work their way through all the
length of Grub Street before they could find an
outlet to success.

How much of unqualified autobiography there
is in "The Wind and the Rain" is more than I can
say. There may be some romance in the charming
chronicle of his first love—his innocent boyish
passion for the little office girl, Gracie Scott, a
perfect idyll till it reached its pitiful ending. And
there may be some romance in the later story of
his love for the tantalising Cicely who will neither
accept or definitely reject him, but plunges him
into despair at last. Anyhow, it is significant that
writing in the first person he gives the narrator no
surname, and lets Cicely slip into calling him
"Tommy" when they are talking together; and
while he is doing all he can to make the best of
himself and impress her favourably, "With two
pounds that I had received for a story," he writes,
"I printed twenty copies of my poems in booklet
form for her." In one of his recent essays, with

slight variations, incidentally making the girl much younger, he repeats that about his printing the booklet for her, and it happens that before I met Burke I had picked up one of those twenty copies on a second-hand stall for twopence—a thin pamphlet in a grey paper cover, with "Verses" for its modest title. In pursuance of my lawful occasions, reviewing "The Wind and the Rain", I referred to my possession, and Burke wrote and confessed that it was the booklet of which he had written and lamented that he had lost his copy and never been able to light upon another. As it seemed intolerable that I should keep mine while the author had none, I reluctantly followed the example of Sir Philip Sidney, and when I subsequently told an incurable collector what I had done he used harsh words about me, saying he would have paid me handsomely for it, and making as if he would tear the hair from his head, but I expect he had already suffered too many such disappointments, for he had none left.

Even more than in his novels and stories, I think you may come to a close acquaintance with Burke's history, his personality and idiosyncrasies, in certain of his essays and sketches, particularly those "Nights in Town", in whose opening essay, "Nocturne", he says, "As a born Londoner, I cannot remember a time when London was not part of me, and I part of London. . . .

THE GLORY THAT WAS GRUB STREET

"And always it is London by lamplight which I vision when I think of her, for it was the London of lamplight that first called to me, as a child. She hardly exists for me in any other mood or dress. It was London by night that awoke me to a sense of that terrible spirit which we call Beauty, to be possessed by which is as unsettling and as sweetly frightful as to be possessed by Love. . . . Open your window when you will in the gloating evening, whether you live in town, in the near suburbs, or in the far suburbs—open your window and listen. You will hear London singing to you; and if you are one of her chosen you will have no sleep that night until you have answered her. There is nothing for it but to slip out and be abroad in the grey, furtive streets, or in the streets loud with lamps and loafers, and jostle the gay men and girls, or mingle with the chaste silences."

That love of London and his intense feeling for the beauty and mystery and terror of her streets by night, when they lie naked under the moon, half lost in fog, or lighted and shadowed by lamps and the shine of shop-windows, finds expression in sensitive, graphic impressions and descriptions that are scattered through all his books. When provincials say as they do, in the pride of discovery, that the born Londoner never knows his own city they are talking of what they do not understand. Unless you were born in London, and have wandered about it from childhood to maturity till your past flows through its streets as the blood through your veins, you may acquire an exhaustive acquaintance with it superficially but will never really know the heart and soul of the place as Burke knows them. He reveals the complexities of its character, its various and varying moods, its homeliness, grimness, squalors, loveliness, with an intimacy and sympathetic insight that are instinctive with him, because he did not approach it as an inquiring stranger but is a child of the city, nurtured and moulded by its associations and influences and mystically at one with it. I have marked several passages that illustrate this, but you can turn them up almost anywhere in his books; my space is dwindling and I want to add one more contribution from "Nocturnal" to my autobiographical fragments:

"When I was a small child I was as other children of our set. I played their games in the street. I talked their language. I shared their ambitions. I worshipped their gods. Life was a business of Board School, breakfast, dinner, tea, struggled for and eaten casually, either at the table or at the door or other convenient spot. I should grow up. I should be, I hoped, a City clerk. I should wear stand-up collars. I might have a moustache. For Sunday I might have a frock coat and silk hat, and, if I were very clever and got on well, a white waistcoat. I should have a house—six rooms and a garden, and I might be able to go to West End theatres sometimes, and sit in the pit instead of the gallery. And some day I might even ride in a hansom cab, though I should have to succeed wonderfully to do that. I hoped I should succeed wonderfully, because then the other boys at the Board School would look up to me."

THE GLORY THAT WAS GRUB STREET

He has done wonderfully, but not exactly on those lines. He became a City clerk, and possibly wore stand-up collars, but if he grew a moustache he has long since removed it. He can't ride in hansom cabs for there are none. I have seen him in the pit and in the stalls at theatres, and he could wear a top hat if he liked, and possibly has done so in special circumstances, but not when I have been looking.

The City clerk, hampered by all sorts of disadvantages, developed into an author and journalist; the periodicals that had too often rejected his contributions not only began to accept them but to ask for more. Some fifteen years ago his earliest books (not counting the little pamphlet of "Verses") made their appearance; these were "The Charm of the West Country", and one or two other anthologies that showed good taste and good judgment in their selections and that he had become a wide and catholic reader. A volume of sketches, "Pavements and Pastures", was followed in 1915 by "Nights in Town", which takes you all over London, from Limehouse to Chelsea, from Whitechapel, Stepney, the Isle of Dogs to Surbiton and Clapham Common, and in its general tone and character was as a shadow cast before them by the books that were to come—except that it was more than a shadow, for it established his reputation and there are things in it that for beauty of thought and style and depth of human interest compare with anything he has written. He continued these "town travels" in "The London Spy", in 1922, but meanwhile with "Limehouse Nights" (1916) and "Twinkletoes" he had risen into popularity as the laureate of London's Chinatown, of those Limehouse byways in which the wily Celestial furtively runs his gambling hells or opium dens, or, like Quong Lee, of "The Wind and the Rain", and of that quaint book of verses "The Song Book of Quong Lee", keeps small gaudily-decorated shops for the sale of tea, jars of ginger, tinned fruit and fish and syrup and such like everyday commodities. One of the "Limehouse Nights" stories, "The Chink and the Child", was turned into a film-play under the title of "Broken Blossom", and was one of the most moving and artistically produced films I have seen. It had a considerable success, in spite of the fact that one of our leading newspapers made a resolute attack upon its idyllic tale of a Chinaman's devout love of a white girl, on the ground that it threw a sentimental glamour over the relations between white women and yellow men in the East End and might have the harmful effect of encouraging the growth of a tendency that often had disastrous consequences. However that may be, there is no denying the pathos, the power or the humour of these romances of Chinatown. They are the more truthful for being melodramatic, for there is always more melodrama than tragedy in human life, especially the life that Burke depicts in these tales and in "East of Mansion House" (1928). But though his Chinatown tales gave him his popularity and his label and inspired a school of imitators, for his best and most enduring work you must go, I think, to his "Nights in Town" and to his two novels, "The Wind and the Rain" and "The Sun in Splendour" (1927). The Islington publican and his musical friends and the rest of the group of characters in this last are drawn, and the whole quietly realistic story told with the same breadth and depth of understanding, sympathetic humour and mature philosophy that are the distinctive qualities of "The Wind and the Rain", and would seem to indicate that Burke has not reduced his art to a formula but is still developing it and will presently have left his "Limehouse Nights", as Dickens left his Boz sketches, behind him—a brilliant background for something bigger.

G.K. CHESTERTON

GILBERT KEITH CHESTERTON

NEARLY every author who knows how to write writes too much, and even Shakespeare could not do this without writing a good deal that was not good enough, and to save him from the consequences his commentators have been driven to prove, from internal evidence, that lesser dramatists were responsible for his worst plays and for the worst parts of some of his best. Authors who do not know how to write also write too much and, if it pays them, there is no reason why they should not, for it cannot do them any harm. But such as bring some genius to their work cannot with impunity allow themselves to be so carelessly prolific. No large quantity of literature from the same pen can keep always at its highest pitch, and the inferior leaven has an effect of watering the general quality of the whole—seems to cloud and diminish what is great in it; as one or two defeats will mar the reputation of an otherwise victorious leader. Time and posterity may readjust things, may reduce an author's garden to order and make its beauty fully manifest; but his contemporaries have to walk there while he is cultivating it, or letting it run wild, and they cannot always see the flowers for the weeds.

Not long ago, at a public debate, I heard an aggressive, too-confident speaker accuse G. K. Chesterton to his face of wasting his great gifts on clever levities. "He takes up any subject and plays with it brilliantly," said this drastic critic, "and at the finish you feel you have been entertained, amused, a little bewildered with paradoxes and fantastically ingenious theories, but you come out at the same door by which you went in and bring nothing with you. It is time Mr. Chesterton began to take himself and his readers seriously. He is too versatile, and has so far done many things cleverly but irresponsibly; he has sacrificed everything to his love of saying what is startling, unorthodox, witty, provocative, and so far has written plenty that has pleased the crowd, but nothing that will live in our literature, and I think he could if he would."

This was impertinent and largely inaccurate; yet there was a grain of truth in it. Chesterton, like most authors, has written too much; he has plunged into controversy in print as well as on the platform; he is a poet and a politician; a philosopher and a writer of detective yarns; a patriot but an opponent of jingoism; a champion of the common man, and glories in the pageantry and feudalism of the Middle Ages; enemy alike of the capitalist system and of

24

Socialism, he carries a banner in the crusade against
all forms of industrial tyranny and political corrup-
tion, and though Capitalists mistake him for a
Socialist, few Socialists make the mistake of supposing he is against them in their resolve to shatter this
unhappy old world, because he is not with them in
their ideal of what it shall be when they have reshaped
it nearer to their heart's desire.   He is an individualist
who could not be contented in a heaven on earth that
was run by even the most perfect machinery, but
would prefer some sort of "Distributive State" in
which private property was not abolished but so
readjusted that every man might have some small
share of his own and be left free to develop it and
himself in his own way.   He is all for individual
liberty, and would not have human beings benignantly
shaped to one seemly, standard pattern, but delights
in their diversity of character, though he is somewhat
intolerant of Jews and a few others and, as a recent
satirist says in "A Little Pilgrim's Peeps at Parnassus", is apt to

> "Set up a chanticleering shrill
> From Campden Hill to Notting Hill,
> And chase to deeps of livid hells
> Teetotallers and infidels."

It is not these minor inconsistencies—for there
are minor inconsistencies in all our philosophies—
that perplex some of his admirers, but his practice of

expressing simple truths in terms of paradox, of
putting on the motley and seeming to treat all life
as a riotous jest, and then by a sudden translation
showing that the jest had a profoundly earnest meaning, that it was full of laughter only as a sky is full
of sunlight, and the dazzle of it half hid and half
revealed spiritual significances for which a more
conventional prophet might have found staider but
not such beautiful or suggestive utterance. People
less nimble-witted than himself are bewildered and
resentful when his joke startles and takes them
unawares by turning into a sermon before they have
fairly got hold of it. I remember how some of
his earliest critics protested against these surprises
and, instead of realising that he was deeply sincere
and only edged his loftiest, most spiritual teaching
with fantasy and humour, as mediæval builders, with
a joyous reverence, edged their churches with gar-
goyles, urged him to subdue his flippancies and
treat serious subjects with due seriousness. If he
could have had his sense of humour removed and
taken their advice I think, by now, he would be
more widely recognised than he is as a great mystic,
an inspired visionary, a profound and original thinker,
for in this country a settled gravity and something of
dullness and, preferably also, a chin full of whiskers
(though there is no salvation in whiskers without
gravity, as Shaw has discovered) are accepted as

evidences of wisdom, and laughter as nothing but a sign of shallowness or folly.

And yet without their subtleties of wit, their Puckish, whimsical commentary on life and the ways of the world, how much of beauty and significance would be lost from many of Chesterton's books—from the revealing allegory of "The Ball and the Cross", for example, and from that most brilliant of his novels, "The Napoleon of Notting Hill", which, with its glorification of suburban patriotism, seems all through the first half of it sheer burlesque and riotous nonsense, and then with a swift touch, toward the close, all that burlesque and nonsense is interpreted and transformed, as by magic, and becomes poignantly fine and full of meaning. You may say this method is nothing but clever artifice and fantastically extravagant, but there is a curiously simple naturalness at the heart of it for are we not most of us consoling ourselves amid the apparent follies, futilities, grotesque ambitions, happy failures and miserable successes of human existence with a thought that, in the end, the purpose of this blended farce and tragedy will be made clear to us and what had seemed ludicrous or trivial will take on the grandeur of being an indispensable part in an ordered and magnificent design?

You get a good deal of the true inwardness of the Chestertonian philosophy in his series of little essays,

"The Defendant". I am not denying that there is occasional perversity in them, some utterances of momentary moods that are buoyantly insisted upon as if they were permanent opinions; but even while you are calling his arguments in defence of farce, nonsense, heraldry, and other things, nonsensical, because they are unorthodox, you are aware that there is a disturbing truthfulness at the core of them. You may fail to rise to Chesterton's mediæval ideals, but, in the matter of heraldry, you have to admit that "there is something to be said for the peculiar influence of pictorial symbols on men's minds", that everything pictorial "suggests, without naming or defining. There is a road from the eye to the heart that does not go through the intellect." And here, from that same "Defence of Heraldry", is an epitome of the social gospel pervading much of "The Napoleon of Notting Hill":

"In the old aristocratic days there existed this vast pictorial symbolism of all the colours and degrees of aristocracy. When the great trumpet of equality was blown, almost immediately afterwards was made one of the greatest blunders in the history of mankind. For all this pride and vivacity, all these towering symbols and flamboyant colours, should have been extended to mankind. The tobacconist should have had a crest, and the cheesemonger a war-cry. The grocer who sold margarine as butter should have felt that there was a stain on the escutcheon of the Higginses. Instead of doing this, the democrats made the appalling mistake—a mistake at the root of the whole modern malady

—of decreasing the human magnificence of the past instead of increasing it. They did not say, as they should have done, to the common citizen, 'You are as good as the Duke of Norfolk,' but used that meaner democratic formula , 'The Duke of Norfolk is no better than you are'."

That passion for romance and a feeling for the underlying dignity and happiness of it are the common bond that links Chesterton's books up one with another through all their wide diversity of theme, his "Life of St. Francis" with the unconventionally sensational stories of "Father Brown" and "The Man Who Was Thursday"; "The Ballad of St. Barbara" and the tale of "The Flying Inn" with his "Short History of England", which hampered itself with no dates, and his "What I saw in America"; the frivolity of "Greybeards at Play" with the vision and profound suggestiveness of "The Everlasting Man", his early "Heretics" with his later "The Uses of Diversity". He has been named the laughing philosopher, and there is more wisdom in his laughter, a deeper knowledge and human sympathy, than in the merely bookish philosopher who impresses the unthinking with his dead weight of learning but has never come out of his study and grown familiar enough with life itself to be on laughing terms with it.

Chesterton has grown familiar with life, yet it seems never to have lost its morning freshness for him; he still goes adventuring into it and finds new things everywhere, or sees the old things from a new angle. After all the books that had been written about Dickens, he wrote one that went to the heart of Dickens's secret and gave us a new revelation of him. And though he and Bernard Shaw are mentally and temperamentally poles asunder, in his critical study of Shaw he comes to the subject as independently as if it were hitherto untrodden ground, and pierces to the essential qualities of the man and the strength and weakness of his philosophy with an almost uncanny insight. Always, in Chesterton's best work, there is that sense of seeing everything intensely, vividly, for himself and for the first time, as if for him, as for Traherne's boy,

"Strange treasures lodged in this fair world appear,
Strange all and new to me."

"Everything has in fact another side to it," he writes; and often his paradoxes—those paradoxes that exasperate many of his critics—are nothing but the other side of a too-easily accepted truth, and are not less true but more startling, because they disturb us in our comfortable contemplation of the side which happened to be uppermost and we had not before turned over. Anyhow, he is himself his greatest paradox: he has the unwieldy bulk of Dr. Johnson and the eager soul of Don Quixote;

something of the robust drollery of Falstaff is in his humour, and the lightness and nimble, glancing spirit of Ariel in his wit; he will turn from writing leading articles on modern politics, the chicanery of politicians, the divorce laws, to fight for a dream, an ideal of heaven on earth, with all the ardour and romantic chivalry that belonged to the day of the knights of the Round Table; he will debate on a platform about practical economics, and, according to his earliest biographer, he used to walk London carrying a sword-stick, yearning for a wild hour in which he might use it gallantly.

Withal, he was born in the staid suburb of Kensington in the year 1874 of the decorous Victorian era. From St. Paul's School he went to begin life tamely as a clerk in an office; but he was not made for "that dry drudgery at the desk's dead wood." His first ambition led him to study at the Slade School; and that he studied to good purpose his latter-day illustrations in some of Belloc's books bear witness. But before long he exchanged the pencil for the pen and instead of practising art began to criticise it in the pages of the *Bookman;* and presently was contributing art and literary criticism and essays on all things under the sun to the *Daily News* and other of the dailies and weeklies. Then came his first book, "The Wild Knight", a book of poems; and in the quarter of a century since the books he has added to that—poetry, essays, histories, biographies, novels, short stories, books on art and of travel—number already over two score. This, to say nothing of his work as editor of the *New Witness*, and later of *G. K. C.'s Weekly* in which he has found opportunity to bring that sword-stick into play, metaphorically speaking, and attacked public wrongs, the social and political evils of his generation, lustily, with a courage and disregard of his own interests that have made him many enemies and, I think, more friends.

CLEMENCE DANE.

CLEMENCE DANE

THE stage seems to have an almost irresistible fascination for the novelist. Sooner or later, having dramatised one of his stories or written an entirely new play, he goes to it and has to have half a dozen failures before he turns his back on it and makes a dignity of his disaster by explaining that the drama to-day has sunk to such a low level that he cannot bring himself to climb down to it. If he meets with a resounding success, however, he probably transforms himself, at once or after a short interval, into an all-time dramatist and writes no more novels. That has been the way with Sir James Barrie, with Bernard Shaw and A. A. Milne. There are a few novelists who, after establishing themselves successfully in the theatre, go on practising the two arts more or less alternatively. Somerset Maugham does that, and Eden Phillpotts, and Alan Monkhouse, and St. John Ervine. Whether there is wisdom in this divided allegiance may be a matter of opinion, but in general there is a good deal to be said for Andrew Marvell's aspiration:

THE GLORY THAT WAS GRUB STREET

"Let us roll all our strength and all
Our sweetness up into one ball"——

for the greatest artists have concentrated their genius
on one art, and I do not remember that any man
ever achieved an equal mastery of two.

So far, Miss Clemence Dane looks like proving
one of the exceptions. Such novels as "Regiment
of Women" and "Legend" have given her place
among the best of contemporary novelists, and
such plays as "Bill of Divorcement" and "Will
Shakespeare" among the best of contemporary
dramatists; and it is not for me to speculate on
whether she will reach her highest self-expression
by concentrating exclusively on this medium or
that or continuing to practise both. Since her
success in the theatre she seemed to have discontinued writing novels, but has returned to fiction
and written some long short stories in which
condensed form of narrative, the arts of dramatist
and novelist were successfully combined. I was
going to say she began as a novelist, but she was
doing other things before that beginning.

Brought up in the country and educated at three
big schools in England, after spending a year in
Dresden, Miss Clemence Dane went as teacher at
a French school in Geneva when she was sixteen.
Thereafter, she had three years at the Slade School,
studying painting, and another year of painting at

34

Dresden. She had intended making portrait painting her profession, and for several years did a good deal of poster work, but, much as she liked it, she had to give up the idea of living by her brush because, as she once confessed, "it did not pay very well ".

Following a further period of school teaching, she went on the stage for four or five years, played all manner of parts on tour, and at the Criterion created the part of Vera Lawrence in Mr. and Mrs. Esmond's "Eliza Comes to Stay", for which production she also painted the posters. Soon after the commencement of the war her health broke down, so she left the stage and then, with the advice and help of the friend "E.A.", to whom she dedicated "Regiment of Women", tried her hand at fiction. Apart from certain tentative efforts in her schoolgirl days, that first novel of hers was her first attempt at producing literature; though she had all along been an inveterate reader of anything and everything in the way of books and magazines, from Bergson to the *Boy's Own Paper*.

From memories of her schooldays, or of those girls' schools in which she served as a teacher, she drew a vividly, minutely realised background for "Regiment of Women"—a first novel so free of immaturities, so sure in its knowledge of character, its sense of drama and of style, you read it with a feeling that here was no novice trying a 'prentice

35

hand but one who had studied life and letters before
she started to write and came fully equipped to the
work she had set herself to do. The central figure
of the story is the strange, masterful woman, Clare,
whose sinister power over the timorous young girl
who falls under her influence is only broken when
the girl meets with an ordinary, sensible, good
man and her love of him casts out her fear of
Clare.

This first book in 1917 was no false dawn, and
Miss Clemence Dane went on into her day next
year with "First the Blade"—a comedy of growth,
of the hopes and errors and charming follies of youth
and love, touched with poignance and something
of disillusion when romance is brought up against
realities, with more of humour in it and perhaps
even more of truth to normal human experience
than its predecessor had. In 1919 came "Legend",
and in 1924 "Wandering Stars", a story of the
theatre, of an actress who off the stage is an ordinary,
homely, lovable woman, who loves with the purest
whole-heartedness the dramatist who has written a
a play for her but can never understand her because
he imagines he understands women and mistakes
even their simplicities for complexes. When she
is acting she can make him see her as any woman
she pleases, and her tragedy is that, when she is not
playing a part, "I can't make him see me as myself"

36

CLEMENCE DANE

He has written a play for her in which he wants her to create the part of a woman who is in love with three men, and she loathes the idea of it and, loving him and him only, cannot believe that a woman can be so "promiscuous".

That is where Miss Clemence Dane differs from so many modern novelists who handle what has come to be named the problem of sex. She is as essentially modern as the most advanced of them, but her knowledge of feminine human nature is wider and deeper. She knows that the ancient sanctities of love between the sexes are still as real as are those cat and dog instincts over which some men and women seem to have little or no control; instincts which only seem more prevalent now than they used to be because they are indulged more openly. When they are necessary to her theme she handles that sort of man and woman, in her novels and plays, with the dispassionate faithfulness of the artist, but she never writes, as do some of the novelists who strain after seeming very doughtily modern, as if decency and self-restraint and a sensible recognition that human creatures no longer go about on four legs, like the rest of the animals, had gone out of fashion and were passing away with the last of the Victorians. Women of easy virtue and lecherous men are as common now as they were in Restoration days or when the Prince

Regent set the pace, and the novelist who fills his book with these does not prove how much but how little he knows of the world at large. He despises those authors who write goody-goody religious novels, but his pictures of life and character are as partial and untrue as theirs, he is as bigoted and narrowly limited in one extreme as they are in another; as literature his work and theirs is equally valueless and in the end they share the same ragbag between them.

Miss Clemence Dane is not afflicted with such deplorable limitations. Airs from heaven and blasts from a different quarter are in the wind that blows about her world, whose people are good and bad, clean and dirty, base and noble, weak and strong, pitiful and contemptible as people really are in the only world that any of us know. You get various samples of them in that group of literary and artistic persons who meet at the house of Anita Serle, in "Legend". The one woman of genius among them, Madala Grey, has married and dropped out of the circle, but her fine personality still dominates them, and they meet and drift into discussing her, and it is from their talk that you come to know her with a curious intimacy, for she never enters the story in person, and is dead soon after it begins. Anyone who has been much in literary society will be familiar with the types that figure in that group. There is the complacent, imperturbable Miss Howe and the gushing, rather likeable Baxter Girl, who write novels; the charming, innocent Jenny, who writes nothing and is the looker-on who relates what she sees and hears; Anita, who has failed as a novelist but has become a critic of considerable influence, and credits herself with a deeper insight of human psychology than she possesses; the artist Kent, who may be no saint but has enough sincerity and greatness of heart to make him wholesome and even admirable; and the cynical, self-satisfied Jasper Flood with his dubious Blanche—Jasper who "wrote reviews and very difficult poetry that didn't rhyme"; he has no faith in human nature, will not believe that Madala Grey, who is in herself, for all her genius, a normal woman, has married a country doctor wholly for love and settled down happily to domesticity. He suggests she has married for "copy"; he will give her a year and then she will tire of it and be back with them; he hints that Kent has been her lover, that there have probably been others. Everybody knows his kind—one of those confirmed slugs who leave a slimy trail over every reputation they come across.

Through the loose, flippant, witty, sometimes scandalous sometimes sympathetic talk, the recollections and opinions of this group, you come

to know both the actual Madala and the very
different Madala who will probably become known
to the public, for Anita, who "discovered" her,
fostered her gift and "made her", is going to write
her biography, and it is the Madala created by
these gossipers who will get into that book, and not
the true woman. She was nothing but "a sort of
star" to them, "symbol—a legend", and as the
little Jennie says to Kent, when he sits apart from
the rest, broken with grief at the news of Madala's
death—for he had loved her though she had not
loved him—"She wasn't like that. She was just a
girl. She was hungry all the time. She was wanting
her human life. And he, the man they laugh at,
'the thing she married,' he did love that real Madala
Grey. Why, he didn't even know of the legend.
Don't you see that that was what she wanted? She
could take from him as well as give. Life—the
bread and wine—they shared it. Oh, and it's him
I pity now, not you."

With all their humour and irony, Miss Clemence
Dane's novels always look on life from a woman's
point of view. I may think "Legend" the most
brilliant, the most subtle of the four in its psychology,
but they differ too much in idea and in manner for
profitable comparison; and there are these same
differences in her plays, for she is not one of those
authors who work in a groove. "The Way Things

Happen" is a successful experiment in melodrama,
though it was only half successful on the stage. Its
problem and its homely realism give "A Bill of
Divorcement" a more poignantly emotional appeal,
the pathos and spiritual tragedy of it grow so naturally
out of the characters of the unloved husband, divorced
during his long insanity and unexpectedly recovered,
the submissive, sensitive, Victorian-minded woman
who shrinks from being unkind to him, and would
have taken him back, though she was on the verge
of marriage with the man she loves, and her very
charming but practical twentieth-century daughter,
Sydney, who "knows too much", and sends her
mother away to happiness, breaks off her own
engagement and devotes herself to her father, feeling
they need each other, they are "both in the same
boat", and marriage and children are not for her.
"Granite", in its wilder atmosphere of eerie
diablerie, is unlike either of these; and her poetical
drama, "Will Shakespeare", is sheer romance, and
has little enough in common with any of the other
three, except the truth and vividness of its characterisation. In telling the story of Shakespeare, from
his desertion of his wife, Anne, his tramp to London
with the wandering players, to his rise to fame as
a dramatist, Miss Clemence Dane accepts the
theory of his passion for Mary Fitton, the Dark
Lady of the sonnets, gives him Marlowe for rival

in her love, and, boldly taking liberties with historical fact, makes Shakespeare, in a jealous frenzy, kill Marlowe by accident at the Deptford tavern. But she is as much entitled as Shakespeare himself was to alter history to suit her purposes, and all that matters is that she has fashioned it into a glowingly picturesque romantic drama that holds a reader's interest as it held the audiences that went to see it at the Shaftesbury Theatre in 1921; a drama, moreover, that is written mostly in easy, limpid verse that often flowers into graces of fancy and thoughts and pictures of haunting, imaginative and poetical beauty.

In point of time, "The Way Things Happen" and "Granite" came later than "Will Shakespeare", and whether she will return to the poetical drama, as I hope she will, or to realistic drama of the comedies and tragedies of modern life, or to the novel, which I hear is her present intention—all this is on the knees of the gods. She does not turn out novels or plays annually; when most authors have been ten years before the public you begin to feel that you can safely place them in their particular niche, but you cannot feel that with Miss Clemence Dane, for she follows no beaten track, and you can never be sure that you will find her again where you left her last.

THEODORE DREISER

I HAVE never quite made up my mind whether a literary censorship is or is not to be desired; the only decision I have been able to arrive at is that, however good it may be for those who like it, I should strongly resent having anybody vested with such authority over myself. I prefer to select my own reading, and if you have noticed how frequently competent critics disagree about the merits of many books, you may reasonably doubt whether any man, or group of men, is qualified to exercise a dictatorship in these matters and spoon-feed the rest of us. Of course, you will say, it would be the sole business of a literary censor to ban books upon ethical grounds; but when you remember that, to say nothing of others, Shaw's "Mrs. Warren's Profession" or "Widower's Houses" (or was it both?) and "The Showing Up of Blanco Posnet" lay for long under the ban of a censor, you will suspect that the judgment of no one mortal of us all is to be trusted, even to that limited extent.

Many were shocked at Ibsen a generation ago, but who to-day would blush to be found reading him?

43

THE GLORY THAT WAS GRUB STREET

I am old enough to remember when Vitzetelly was prosecuted and imprisoned for translating and publishing Zola in this country, but I don't think we are nowadays proud of that episode. More recently, the premises of a famous publishing house were raided by the police, who confiscated all copies of a novel by an author who has since become famous. It was a novel of the unhealthy sort that soon dies a natural death if you leave it alone; but as a result of that sensational suppression a society was formed whose members in return for an annual subscription of ten guineas had that special book and others supplied to them privately. You can never suppress that sort of thing by driving it underground; it usually flourishes longer there than it would have done if you had left it to look paltry and wilt in the common cleanness of the sunlight. Anyhow, they are a small minority of authors who devote themselves to writing such *jejune* stuff, as they are a small minority of crude minds that find congenial expression in obscene words and drawings scribbled on convenient walls. There is really nothing to choose between those literary and these mural artists, and the public which, in the main, is sensible and decent-minded, silently, unostentatiously censures both with an equal contempt.

No other and more limited censorship can, I am afraid, be trusted. Some well-meaning men can see nothing but wrong in any fiction that touches, however sincerely and with whatever high artistic or moral purpose, on the relations between the sexes. One does not forget the reception accorded to Hardy's " Tess " and " Jude the Obscure ", and in this present year of grace a powerful censorship which has been set up in a leading American city has banned a large number of English and American novels. The American *Authors' League Bulletin* says that though the censorship is unofficial "it is regarded with terror by booksellers," who, as soon as they are notified of the names of books considered objectionable, withdraw them from sale. The novels banned in what the *Bulletin* calls "the latest wholesale gesture of terrorisation" include St. John Ervine's " The Wayward Man ", Warwick Deeping's " Doomsday ", Adelaide Eden Phillpotts's "Tomek the Sculptor", and Theodore Dreiser's "The American Tragedy". One or two of the other books on this precious list may be open to question; I have named only such as I have read, and what any mature man or woman can have discovered in any of these that could be harmful to a reader of average intelligence passes my comprehension.

No greatly gifted novelist of our time has been more stupidly misjudged than has Theodore Dreiser. The prudes of some thirty years ago as grossly misunderstood his first novel, "Sister Carrie", as the fewer prudes of to-day have grossly misunderstood

45

his latest, "The American Tragedy". When "Sister Carrie" was published in America in 1900 it was so fiercely attacked on moral grounds, very much as "Tess" had been fulminated against here a few years earlier, that it was promptly withdrawn from publication. As Mr. Percy Holmes Brynton tells you in his "More Contemporary Americans", in 1911 "Theodore Dreiser's 'Jennie Gerhardt' was published and received with acclaim; before the applause subsided it was discovered that eleven years agone his 'Sister Carrie' had been published and sup-pressed—auto-suppressed—without exciting attention by either event. When reprinted it was applauded as vigorously as the companion book." Meanwhile, well before the war, "Sister Carrie" and one or two other of Dreiser's novels were issued in this country, but though our critics were not slow to recognise the knowledge and truth and insight of human character that was in them, so far as I recollect our public gave them no enthusiastic reception. Possibly, English readers were deterred by vague memories of the abuse that had been showered upon "Sister Carrie" in America; and, as Dreiser is certainly not a novelist to satisfy the particular (or not very particular) readers for whom the puerile indecencies of excusably banned books are written, it is possible that here at that date he rather fell between the two stools.

46

THEODORE DREISER

However, that is all left behind us; we have broadened our literary and other horizons and changed many of our views since then. Dreiser, in the interval, has continued to go his own way, till the reading world is at length going after him. He is no longer a prophet without honour in his own country; when, in 1925, his latest and most masterly story, "The American Tragedy", appeared over there I suppose it became apparent to most people that he is about the greatest thing in novelists modern America has produced. And this impression was confirmed in 1927 when Constables began to publish a collected edition of his novels on this side of the Atlantic.

Born in 1871, Theodore Dreiser started as a reporter on the *Chicago Globe* in 1892. On that and other newspapers he did his full tale of journalistic work, as travelling correspondent, as dramatic editor; successively edited three popular magazines, and since 1907 has been editor-in-chief of the well known Butterick publications. If all these activities prevented him from being a novelist of leisure, they kept him closely in touch with the everyday life of his time, and gave him the intimate knowledge of it that he puts with such casual-seeming realism into his stories. You suspect that if he had not himself endured humiliations and suffered vicissitudes he could scarcely have described in such minute detail and with such intensity of feeling the vicissitudes and humiliations some of his characters have to endure. He does not merely tell you that Sister Carrie had a long and heart-breaking search for work, but takes you with her, trudging through the roaring city, nervously invading one busy shop after another, sometimes walking once or twice past the door before she can steel herself to go in; to be snubbed, or brusquely rebuffed, or to have her disappointment mitigated by a plain businesslike courtesy or some touch of kindly regret—through all the hopeless quest, to the hard and ill-paid job she takes on with an eager thankfulness at last, you go every inch of the way with her and are made to realise to the full how her courage is worn down, her innate rectitude overtried and weakened, till the genial, plausible Charles Drouet finds it comparatively easy at last to persuade her into the pleasanter way that he opens to her. The power of this and of all Dreiser's stories lies in their quiet naturalness; circumstance and incident combine to make the whole thing inevitable; it may be regrettable, but that is how it happened— that is how it does happen and has happened in the actual world which his fiction faithfully reflects.

He is not much of an idealist, for he sees through the shows of things—sees them starkly as they are, and simply writing the mere truth of them as he sees it, with a practical, worldly-wise philosophy, has no choice but to be a "stern moralist" in the sound old Puritan meaning of the term. He has no charm of style; puts no gilt edge on vice; does not (like some of our uncensored novelists) treat illicit love as a matter for farcical comedy, or as a rational and satisfactory form of amusement for men and women who are too clever to be conventional: he knows too much of life to misinterpret it in that superficial fashion. I wish that, one day, Dreiser would give us the complete history of the Walterses, those "kind and gentle and orderly people" at whom he glances in "Chains", or of "young Mrs. Justus", in the same book, "a simple, home-loving little woman who would never dream of the treacheries and eccentricities of Idelle", as the distracted Garrison says to himself, thinking of his unreliable wife while he watches Mrs. Justus coming from her house opposite. These orderly, homely folk have a large place in human society, and should have a larger place in Dreiser's world than he has so far given them.

Otherwise, he pictures everywhere the difficulties and complexities of life in big cities (in Chicago, Philadelphia, New York) with a wonderfully realistic intimacy. When young Cowperwood, of "The Financier", goes into business, you are brought to know everything about that business through all its ramifications; when he goes on 'Change, you are exhaustively informed of the meaning of Stock

Exchange terms, of precisely what he does there, and how he does it. The whole inner workings of his mind are as minutely revealed, and from his youth, when he had "no consciousness of sin", was indifferent to considerations of good and evil, had no belief in anything but strength and weakness: if you were strong you could take care of yourself, do what you liked, be something; if you were weak, you must keep out of the way or submit to whatever may happen to you; he cares for nothing but to succeed, to make money, to dominate others—from his youth, when these are his only principles, you follow his gradual development, his rise, his brilliant progress, his lapse into the failure and disgrace that naturally result from a self-confidence so arrogant, a self-indulgence so callous and unrestrained. "What wise man," you are asked, "might not read from such a a beginning such an end?" No author whose work needs censoring would have been moved to drive home the grim lesson of sorrow and disillusion that is so movingly epitomised in the closing paragraph of "The Financier".

There is the same sheer sincerity, the same moral earnestness in "Sister Carrie" and in "The American Tragedy". Yet you have a feeling that Dreiser is not out to moralise; he is simply out to tell a plain story of life as he knows it, and, since you literally cannot play with fire without getting burned, the moral is unavoidable because it is implicit in his uncompromising record of what he has observed. He does not preach or indignantly protest or sit in judgment on the crudest or most accomplished of his sinners; but spares you nothing, gives you all the facts, and by impartially unravelling the intricacies of their psychology helps you to understand and judge them for yourself. He handles the worst of them with a charity that is wider than the wideness of the sea, with an instinctive pity alike for their follies and futilities and for the sufferings of those who are wronged by them. I know of no fiction that is more touched with beauty by that pervading sense of pity than are certain parts of "The American Tragedy", and "Sister Carrie", and, especially, that exquisite short story "Sanctuary", in "Chains".

As a realist Dreiser has affinities with Defoe and with Dostoievsky—he has the same direct narrative method, the same undecorated style and, as they do, relies for his effectiveness, not on selecting salient incidents, events, characteristics, but on conscientiously piling up every little detail of circumstance affecting his people or their history. Except that he is never grotesque or extravagant in his humour, he has curious affinities, too, with Hogarth—he is as frankly, unreservedly realistic, and has the same severe, practical moral tendency as you find in those series of pictures "The Harlot's Progress", "Industry and Idleness" and "The Rake's Progress". When his people outrage the moral and other social laws they invariably come, as Hogarth's do, to a disastrous ending; and I cannot better summarise what I have been attempting to say of the one than by repeating what Lamb wrote of the other:

"Of the severer class of Hogarth's performances enough I trust, has been said to show that they do not merely shock and repulse; that there is in them the 'scorn of vice' and the 'pity' too; something to touch the heart and keep alive the sense of moral beauty; the *lacrymae rerum*, and the sorrowing by which the heart is made better. If they be bad things, then is satire and tragedy a bad thing; let us proclaim at once an age of gold, and sink the existence of vice and misery in our speculations; let us
'wink and shut our apprehensions up
From common sense of what men were and are;'
let us *make believe* with the children that everybody is good and happy."

Unfortunately we cannot put right what is wrong by closing our eyes to it, nor can we remedy the evils he exposes by stoning the prophet; though some of us seem optimistic enough to go on trying.

ST. JOHN ERVINE

I HAVE been told that St. John Ervine is a typical
Irishman; and that he is not a typical Irishman,
and I don't think he can be, for, so far as my personal
investigations have gone, no Irishman ever was.
The typical Irishman has come down to us like the
wonderful but intangible Mrs. Harris and, in the
words of Betsey Prig, "I don't believe there's no
sich person." Shaw is not one, nor is Yeats, not
A. E., nor George Morrow, nor George Moore,
nor Robert Lynd, nor Arthur Lynch nor Bohun
Lynch, nor is Frankfort Moore, nor Patrick MacGill,
nor Shaw Desmond, nor Coulson Kernahan, nor
any other Irishman I have ever met. Some of them
have slight or rich brogues, but, then, so have some
Scotsmen, and so have many who were born in the
north of England; and, apart from that quite
superficial distinction, I have known Englishmen,
even Cockneys, very much like those Irishmen in
appearance, in temperament, in all essential qualities.
There are all sorts of people in every nation, and you
can match each sort in every other nation, which is
significant enough as evidence of the common

THE GLORY THAT WAS GRUB STREET

brotherhood of man without laying too much stress on the fact that the family is always quarrelling.

Ervine is an Ulsterman; he was born, in 1883, at Belfast, where his father was a printer; but he came to London at the beginning of this century when he was about seventeen and was for a while a clerk in an insurance office, turning his hand to literature in his spare time. The insurance office does not seem to have held him very long. He was a Socialist and, like so many of the younger literary men of that period, a member of the Fabian Society, proved himself able in debate, and took a lively interest in whatever social and political movements were going. Having passed the usual lions that lurk in the path of the literary free-lance, he began to arrive as a journalist, reviewing and writing articles for the *Manchester Guardian*, *Daily News*, and other papers, and presently was made dramatic critic of the *Daily Citizen*. Gerald Cumberland who was on the staff of the *Citizen* with him, said he was not popular with the staff, that he was "very high-brow", that "his face was smooth, sleek and superior, and he had a habit of being friendly with a man one day and scarcely recognising him the next"; and described Ervine as, like Shaw, "a typical Irishman: a fellow who, despite his imagination and sympathy, lives with one eye on the Muse and the other on the cashbox"

54

ST. JOHN ERVINE

That preoccupation is not typical of the natives of any country; Shakespeare's, Scott's, Dickens's eyes, and the eyes of numerous other authors, great and small, of all nationalities, have been similarly engaged, and it indicates nothing worse than that they were not too superior to have a little horse-sense. However this may be, Cumberland's portrait, in his "Set Down in Malice", is in other respects at variance with my own impressions. I first came across St. John Ervine in those days, and to me he seemed extraordinarily sensitive, curiously shy, and I suspect it was this sensitiveness and shyness, not any high-brow proclivities or sense of superiority, that prevented him from making friends easily of everybody. He took his work seriously, was in earnest about it, had no particular leanings, I should say, toward Bohemianism, expressed his opinions and went his way with a certain independence, which is still characteristic of him, and has grown more certain, was never too fearful of giving offence, nor over-anxious to cultivate the goodwill of anybody, important or otherwise, in whose society he found no pleasure. He has not the gift of letting himself go; when he does so you feel he is doing it deliberately, and not because he cannot help it. I do not think he lets himself go often enough even in his writings; but he no more cultivated this restraint than Lamb cultivated his stammer or

Byron his club-foot—it happens to be natural to him. What some have mistaken for intellectual arrogance is nothing but the habitual air of aloofness that envelops one who has no strong gregarious instincts or seldom indulges them. He has more wit than humour, and his humour frequently has teeth in it and bites ironically. He is a realist with a feeling for romance; a sentimentalist at heart, whose native reticence and artistic sensibility regulate any utterance of his emotion.

Before the war broke in upon all peaceful pursuits Ervine was already well known as a dramatist. Between 1910 and 1916 three of his plays (all written before 1914)—"The Magnanimous Lover", "Mixed Marriage", and "John Ferguson"—were produced at the Abbey Theatre, Dublin, and one, "Jane Clegg", at the Gaiety Theatre, Manchester. His later dramas include "The Ship", "Mary, Mary, Quite Contrary", and "The Lady of Belmont", a rather daring, brilliantly satirical continuation of the story of Shylock in which he develops the Jew that Shakespeare drew into a gracious figure of toleration and pathos. Of recent years "John Ferguson" and "Jane Clegg" have been produced with considerable success in London, and "John Ferguson" and "Mary, Mary, Quite Contrary" have had immensely successful runs in America.

ST. JOHN ERVINE

Meanwhile, however, after acting as manager of the Abbey Theatre in 1915, Ervine went on active service as a trooper in the Household Battalion, and in 1917 became a Lieutenant of the Royal Dublin Fusiliers. Fighting on the French front in May, 1918, he was so seriously wounded that he was invalided out of the Army, and presently began to take up the threads of his literary career again. Not that the war had altogether broken them; "John Ferguson", was, as I have indicated, produced in 1916, and in 1917 his second novel, "Changing Winds", written a year or so earlier, made its appearance.

Ervine began as a dramatist, and though as dramatist and dramatic critic he may have a little obscured himself as a novelist, his five novels, "Mrs. Martin's Man", "Changing Winds", "Alice and a Family", "The Foolish Lovers", and "Wandering Men", are sufficient in themselves to have given him a considerable reputation. So far as my own judgment goes, I would rank the two first of these and his plays, "John Ferguson" and "Jane Clegg" as, in their different kinds, his highest achievement in imaginative literature. "Alice and a Family", in lighter vein, is a witty comedy of London life with a charming leaven of sentiment; and I am keenly appreciative of the subtle art, the shrewdly satirical humour and ripe philosophy of "The Lady of

57

Belmont"; but stronger in their human appeal and more characteristic of Ervine's quality are those realistic novels and dramas that find their characters and scenes round about Belfast or in Dublin, and whose stories are racy of the soil of his own country. There is good, soundly capable work in his book of short tales and sketches, "Eight O'Clock"; in his studies of "The Organised Theatre", and of "Sir Edward Carson and the Ulster Movement"; in his searching and brilliant presentation of the career and character of Parnell; and in his delightfully intimate and sometimes devastatingly outspoken reminiscences, "Some Impressions of My Elders"; but on the whole you classify him as a dramatist and novelist, and put down such books as these as in the nature of "extra turns". Even then you have to make additions to his label, for he is one of the most accomplished and influential of present day dramatic critics, and a lecturer who can charm an audience when he will and can chafe it with satirical epigrams and rouse it to indignation when he wants to express opinions that he knows will not be generally acceptable. Just as, a short time back, he exasperated the ladies of Manchester by a lecture in which he commented without flattery on the extent to which women were responsible for the deterioration of the drama—so exasperated them that it was thought necessary to follow him up

58

with another lecturer who attempted to counter his arguments; in the same way, he will not hesitate to move playwrights or players to wrath if he cannot honestly give them applause, though no critic hands out bouquets more generously when he feels he has reason to do that.

He makes his mistakes, like everybody else, but he has the courage of his convictions, even to the extent of forming a new one and publicly discarding the old when he has found it was wrong. As, for instance, when he tells you, in "Some Impressions of My Elders", of one of his many visits to Mr. W. B. Yeats:

"I completed the MS. of 'Mixed Marriage' and, much embarrassed, read it to him in his rooms. I read it very badly, too, and I am sure I bored him a great deal; but he was kind and patient, and he made some useful suggestions to me which I did not accept. I had too much conceit, as all young writers have, to be guided by a better man than myself. I know now that I should have done well to take his advice. He warned me against topical things and against politics and urged me to flee journalism as I would flee the devil; and he advised me to read Balzac. He was always advising me to read Balzac, but I never did."

Earlier than that, he had sent Yeats a play, "Mrs. Martin's Man", hoping he would produce it at the Abbey Theatre, but Yeats wrote him a long letter pointing out that it was "an error", and he put the play in the fire. He admits now that he knows the play "to have been a dreadful mess of motives", and testifies that Yeats's criticism is "especially valuable when it is adverse"; but the play was not altogether destined to destruction for Ervine took the same theme, purged of the faults that had been found in it, and used it, with the same title, for his first novel.

Although "Some Impressions of My Elders" is given over to lively and graphic recollections and opinions of eight well known contemporary authors, it is also a very intimate self-revelation of the personality of its author. There is nothing woolly or indefinite about his portraits of his friends. He is not concerned to please or offend them, but to paint them as he sees them. Looking on them from different aspects, he will touch in their greatnesses and their littlenesses of character with an impartial hand; if he is writing admiringly of one of them on this page, it is possible he will be writing caustically of him on the next. Warm-hearted in his acknowledgment of their gracious qualities, and as careful to note any affectations of superiority and to resent these with a wry sarcasm, he never attempts to be other than perfectly human and natural, and by the time he has done with them his "elders" are left as human and natural as himself, with all their perfections and imperfections on their heads. This thoroughness is characteristic of his literary methods.

ST. JOHN ERVINE

He is a realist in the right sense of the word, and, seeing the goodness and badness that go to the making of men and women, puts it all in, and is sometimes cynical about it and sometimes as charitable as Mrs. Rainey in "Mixed Marriage", when she talks with a wise tolerance of her domineering husband, and thinks that God made woman "acause He saw what a chile a man is".

Now and then he may seem perverse; and possibly is; but his perversities are as native to him as are his sincerities and may be cherished with equal sincerity while the mood for them lasts. Anyhow, he frankly discloses some of them in that book of his "Impressions", as part of his picture of himself. He seems to wonder why clever men and women "actually paid good American money" to hear him lecture, though they probably had views on the subject "that were at least as sound or sounder than mine". He says he thinks the public pay too much tribute to the author; that too much importance is given to the author as author; that a man who puts words together is not entitled to more respect than is given to the man who puts bits of metal together and makes a motor-car. And "I do not know," he says, "why a man who writes books should regard himself as a better man than one who makes butter." He is often not so good, but it takes more thought, imagination, skill, time to make a book than to make butter, and however you look at it the analogy breaks down. The position of the man who makes butter is more that of publisher than of author, for he is entirely dependent on the cow.

SIR EDMUND GOSSE, C.B.

On the 21st September, 1849, the eminent naturalist Philip Henry Gosse made this entry in his Diary: "E. delivered of a son. Received green swallow from Jamacia." The son who arrived in London almost simultaneously with the green swallow (presumably a stuffed or otherwise preserved specimen to be added to the diarist's collection) was Edmund Gosse who, more than half a century later, was to write that most candid of domestic histories, a blend of biography and autobiography, "Father and Son", with its minutely detailed portraits of himself as a youth, his father, his mother, his step-mother, and others of the family circle or of the little world that surrounded it. I remember how when, in 1896, Barrie published that wistful, beautifully frank and tender study of his mother, "Margaret Ogilvy", there were those who lifted deprecating hands and considered such truthfulness in bad taste, and when "Father and Son" came out, in 1907, the same people or others like them, who make a virtue of secretiveness, raised the same stupid outcry against that. But it was that very truthfulness, that complete revelation of one's self and of the minds and hearts of those one had known and loved best, which gave both books their instant, irresistible appeal. Discretion is no virtue in a biographer, and if Boswell had not realised that his biography would not have been so great, so human and alive as it is.

"Father and Son" made its appearance anonymously, and within six months had been thrice reprinted. Nine or ten new impressions or new editions have since been published, and in 1913, after its authorship was acknowledged, the book was crowned by the French Academy. All which was no more than its due; I could not name any book written this century that is likelier to keep an abiding place in our literature. Some years ago when I happened to say to Sir Edmund Gosse that I ranked "Father and Son" above all the rest of his books, he was inclined to dissent and to prefer his "Life and Letters of Donne". But I remain unconverted. The baffling, fantastic, in some ways noble and lovable personality of Donne does not, I think, emerge so vividly and surely from the "Life and Letters" as do the personalities of Congreve, Jeremy Taylor, Coventry Patmore, Swinburne, from the Lives Gosse has written of them. Perhaps because none could portray in words the complex, simple, mystical, worldly character of Donne except one who had known him intimately in the flesh as

SIR EDMUND GOSSE, C.B.

Isaac Walton knew him; perhaps because any subsequent biography must suffer by comparison with that wonderful, inimitable portrait of Donne which Walton drew.

If Gosse had not devoted himself so much to criticism, and become so eminent as a critic, he would be better known as a poet than he is, but in this country when once a writer has been accepted and labelled as of a particular class, whatever he may do in another kind is eyed with suspicion and not considered seriously. There was a potential novelist, too, in the man who wrote "Father and Son", and the novelist has been at his elbow when he was doing some of the ablest of his critical studies. Gosse is essentially a literary artist whose critical gift and whose grace and charm of style are not more significant than is that rarer gift he has, in biography or criticism, of re-creating character, touching in light and shade and physical and mental attributes with such insight and such deft imaginative realism that the portrait, especially when it is of some contemporary with whom he has been familiar, grows lifelike and vital under his hand. It is his distinction that, like Hazlitt, he is a critic and a good deal more. We read Hazlitt now far less for his brilliant criticisms of books than for his glowing, intimately personal essays on life at large, and for those irreplaceable recollections and impressions of Lamb, Coleridge,

Wordsworth, and other of his great contemporaries. And I feel that, without any skill in prophecy, one may say it will be the same in due season with Edmund Gosse. Later generations may turn to new critics, but they will come back to him for what only he can give them—those masterly literary portraits of men of his time that are in the biographies of poets who were his friends, in his "Portraits and Sketches", "Critical Kit-Kats", and other of his volumes of essays.

It is in these re-creations of character from written records or, in the case of contemporaries, from remembrance that the imaginative artist, the potential novelist finds expression; and Gosse has the artist's passion for giving verisimilitude and life to a portrait by painting, without compromise, the truth as he sees it. This truth to the facts, when it happens to be unflattering, is sometimes mistaken for cynicism or ill-nature. There were indignant idealists who protested against certain realistic details Gosse put into his candid and graphic representation of Swinburne; but he was as scrupulously exact in the portrayal of his father, if not in the more formal "Life of Philip Henry Gosse" (1890), in the later and greater "Father and Son", where he was no less unreserved in the presentment of himself as a child and a young man. You have a complete justification of his method when he tells you in a prefatory note that this narrative "in all parts, and so far as the punctilious attention of the writer has been able to keep it so, is scrupulously true. If it were not true in this strict sense, to publish it would be to trifle with those who may be induced to read it." And when you have read it you recognise that there, in his rigid respect for truth, speaks the son of his father.

The household of "Father and Son" grows upon you, while you read that book, as in most ways a typically Victorian household, careful of the respectabilities, and preoccupied with religious beliefs and observances of the strictest and narrowest sort. The father had been a Wesleyan, the mother an Anglican, but claiming an entire freedom of thought in such matters, they could not accept all the teachings of either community. "By a process of selection my Father and my Mother alike had gradually, without violence, found themselves shut outside all Protestant communions, and at last met only with a few extreme Calvinists like themselves on terms of what may almost be called negation—with no priest, no ritual, no festivals, no ornament of any kind, nothing but the Lord's Supper and the exposition of the Holy Scripture drawing those austere spirits into any sort of cohesion. They called themselves 'the Brethren', simply; a title enlarged by the world outside into 'Plymouth Brethren'." In

67

this atmosphere the father pursued his studies in natural history, publishing occasional books, but his religious faith dominated all his activities. The limitations of that life, the noble, the quietly beautiful the quaintly amusing sides of it are made clear to you in the story, which makes clear to you, too, the deep love that held the small family together, and that a stern adherence to the bigotries of its religious code did not prevent it from being "always cheerful and often gay".

It is no use saying there seemed nothing in Gosse's early surroundings to foster a love of literature, for all or any surroundings will serve to do that. He had no young companions and no outdoor amusements; works of fiction were banned from the house, and with the object of instilling a regard for the truth into him he was allowed to read nothing but history, biography, theology, natural history—books that were supposed to deal with nothing but realities: "Never, in all my early childhood did anyone address to me the affecting prelude, 'Once upon a time!' I was told about missionaries, but never about pirates; I was familiar with humming-birds, but I had never heard of fairies. Jack the Giant Killer, Rumpelstiltskin and Robin Hood were not of my acquaintance, and though I understood about wolves, Little Red Riding-hood was a stranger even by name." Once in an attic he found an old trunk lined with pages of a sensational novel and read this, "kneeling on the bare floor, with indescribable rapture". But the idea of a deliberately invented story had been so successfully kept from him he had no idea that this narrative of exciting adventure was not true.

From the age of four or five he had been solemnly dedicated to religious service—"I cannot recollect the time when I did not understand that I was going to be a minister of the Gospel"—and the spiritual pride he felt in the importance that accrued to him from its being known he was set apart for that high destiny is disclosed with a shrewd, wry humour. But he could not always be kept within such straitened bounds; after his mother's death he had to be sent to school, and began to read the books that had hitherto been inaccessible—Shelley, Keats, Shakespeare; was presently writing verse himself, and, still under the influence of his early training, wrote a Shakespearean tragedy "on a Biblical and evangelical subject"; and Shelleyean odes dealing with "the approaching advent of our Lord and the rapture of His saints".

As his mind matured and expanded he began to shake off the restrictions that had bounded his childhood, to think for himself and live more by his own light. The thought of his dedication to the ministry became by degrees irksome and intolerable, and when he had gone to London to begin his career, in correspondence with his father he was moved, not without compunctions, to renounce it altogether; and one of the most poignant things in "Father and Son" is the letter from the father—who, with all his limitations and peculiarities, leaves on you the final impression of "a unique and noble figure"—mourning over the son's apostacy.

In London, he studied and passed examinations for the Civil Service, and in 1867 became Assistant Librarian at the British Museum, where Coventry Patmore was one of his colleagues. In 1875 he left the Museum for the Board of Trade, where he worked beside Austin Dobson. Already, in 1873, he had published his first book, "With Viol and Flute", a collection of his verse, and had followed this with many others in verse and prose, including his Lives of Congreve, Gray, Donne, Jeremy Taylor, and Philip Henry Gosse; his "Gossip in a Library," "Critical Kit-Kats", "Seventeenth Century Studies", a "History of Eighteenth Century Literature", before, in 1904, he went from the Board of Trade to become Librarian of the House of Lords. To continue the even outline of his progress, he was made a C.B. in 1912; retired from the serene environment of the Upper House in 1914, and was in 1925 honoured with a knighthood. Meanwhile, hardly any year had failed to bring us a new book from him, some years bringing two or three, as

SIR EDMUND GOSSE, C.B.

"French Profiles", Lives of Patmore, Sir Thomas
Browne, Swinburne; his Collected Poems in one
volume and his Collected Essays in five; his more
recent books being collections of these causeries one
hesitates to call scholarly, because they carry their
scholarship with a grace of style and a delightfully
gossipy manner which has made them for some years
past down to the week of his death, in 1928, one of
the most popular features in the *Sunday Times*.

Except for that addiction to truth-telling which
has sometimes irritated the friends or strangers
whom it concerned (though on occasion he can
edge the truth with such subtle and delicate irony
that his victim scarcely knows whether he is stroked
or smitten), there is so little trace of his youthful
experiences in his work that one doubts whether,
in his case, the child was father of the man. So far
from being afflicted with any rigid orthodoxy, he
has kept an open mind always for new developments
in literature; he was among the first to champion
Ibsen in England at a time when the name of Ibsen
was anathema to most readers here and to most
critics; and new poets and new writers generally have
often found in him a prompt and helpful mentor.

In the Epilogue to his Collected Poems you find
him hoping he may have length of days, not that
he may look back and say with barren pride that
"the Past alone is deified", but that, though he

may see his "decayed traditions" swept away, he
may also see and hear and welcome the new beauty
and harmonies that shall supersede them:

> "New arts, new raptures, new desires
> Will stir the new-born souls of men;
> New fingers smite new-fashioned lyres,——
> And O! may I be listening then;"

and he was not only listening, but ready with appreciation and encouragement, and patient of the most
bizarre and raw experiments, in pursuit of his resolve
that
> "My faith in beauty shall not fail
> Because I fail to understand."

He even preserved a benign and philosophic
attitude toward the maddest vagaries of the Sitwell
family; he took the chair for them when they had
or were given by their admirers a public lunch on
a notable occasion; but he did not fail, in reviewing
one of their books, to winnow something of beauty
and reality from their eccentricities and artificialities,
nor to expose their crudities and crass affectations
with an irony as smiling and gentle as it was devastating. He told me when last I saw him that his
interest in things was slackening and that he was an
old man, and I felt that for once, at all events, he had
fallen from that virtue of which the young George
Washington has been the only perfect exemplar, for
in spirit he remained young to the last.

PHILIP GUEDALLA

NEARLY all men of letters began by being something else; and the Law, though popularly supposed to have no concern with anything but facts and the whole truth, would seem to have a peculiar power of prompting those who practice it to a yearning for romance; for it has fostered more novelists, poets, dramatists and historians than have been nourished by any other profession. It is disquieting but well known to those who are in the profession or have escaped from it (as I have) that a large number of the solicitors and barristers you meet, stern, practical-looking men as they are, have in their time written poetry, some are incurable, and occasionally publish anonymously dainty little volumes of " Heart Whispers ", " Songs of Passion", or " Day Dreams ". They carefully conceal this weakness, and a client sitting in front of his lawyer, waiting for advice, may watch him knitting his brows and apparently wrestling in thought with a point of law, and never guess that he is really trying to find a rhyme. But to say nothing of such innumerable minors, the solicitor's office, which has, in

73

the last century or so, produced major poets, novelists, biographers, humorists as Charles J. Wells, John Forster, Disraeli, Watts-Dunton and Walter Emanuel, is a wonderful literary incubator, and the barrister's chambers are far more so.

Philip Guedalla, himself a barrister, makes unkind remarks, in one of his " Masters and Men " essays, about the strange jargon, the " impenetrable terminology ", used by lawyers in legal documents, and adds:

"At its best the lawyers' English is a convenient shorthand for the summary statement of complicated matters. But at its worst (and the worst is more often uppermost in human matters) it is a pompous and deliberate mystification, a more impressive variant of the $Ol: menth: pip:$ with which the physician bewilders his patients (and, not infrequently, the chemist). That terminology constitutes the mystery of the lawyers' craft; and it is the long effort to make and keep a mystery of it that hardens those steely eyes, draws down the corners of those mouths, and weighs heavily on those preoccupied feet that pace so gravely, towards lunch time, across the sunshine in the Temple. . . . Once in a century or so a lawyer is discovered who can write English. In the first shock of the discovery he is apt to desert the Temple and to write *Bab Ballads* or *Dolly Dialogues.*"

Or to write novels, as Scott and Stevenson did, and as Galsworthy, Weyman, Dornford Yates, St. John Lucas, Buchan, and a host of others have done. But there is no lack of barristers, besides

74

PHILIP GUEDALLA

Lord Darling and Lord Birkenhead, who discover they can write English and are able to do it triumphantly, in verse or prose, without quitting the Bar, till it is time to go to the Bench. Philip Guedalla is another of that goodly company and, as a literary artist, at least the peer of one of those two and more than the peer of the other, though he is not yet old enough to be admitted into the Peerage.

He was only born in 1889, and showed his natural bent in his nonage by editing a magazine, which he called *The Meteor*, while he was at Rugby. At Oxford he was soon winning distinction as an able speaker and adroit debater at the Union, and as an actor in the O.U.D.S. He was also writing a good deal of verse, and prose of all sorts, and had no sooner celebrated his majority than, in 1911, he published his two first books, " Metri Gratia ", a miscellany of prose and verse, and " Ignes Fatui ", a collection of his parodies. About that time, too, he began to review other people's books for some of the London papers. Meanwhile, he had taken his First in Mods. and his First in Modern History and, leaving Balliol in 1912, came to London with honours thick upon him, to study Commercial and Common Law and eat his dinners in Hall, and was called to the Bar in 1913. A year later he published his third book, and made his debut as a historian with a lucid and scholarly study of " The Partition of Europe: 1715–1815 ". Then came the war, when he was appointed legal adviser first to the War Office Contracts Department, later to the Ministry of Munitions, with an additional burden of strenuous work in connection with industrial reorganisation.

There were no more books till the war was at an end; then, in 1920, came his first in the manner we have come to regard as characteristic of him— " Supers and Supermen: Studies in Politics, History and Letters ", a vivid, witty, shrewdly revealing series of character studies which at once gave him his own place of distinction among such modern artists of literary portraiture as Lytton Strachey, E. T. Raymond and A. G. Gardiner. From this brilliant " carving on cherrystones " he passed to one of the most masterly of his larger histories, " The Second Empire " (1922) with its careful portrait of Napoleon III, wonderfully intimate and alive, its swift sketches of contemporary life and manners, and the broad, easy sweep of a narrative which wings an encyclopædic knowledge of the period with touches of irony and epigrammatic humour and sets the serio-comic figure of Napoleon the Little in a multi-coloured, well-balanced picture of the social and political life of his times. Nobody has invented stories more romantic than are to be found in historical records, and there is no reason,

as Macaulay said, why an historical work should
not be as interesting and entertaining as a novel.
There is no reason, except when it falls into the
hands of great scholars who resolutely treat it as a
scholarly exercise because they have not the creative
imagination and finer gift of writing that would
enable them to make it more than a plodding,
competent matter-of-fact chronicle. Men like Stubbs
and Freeman, for instance, had all the patient application and exhaustive learning necessary to the
task, they could bring together all the material and
with scientific exactness articulate the anatomy of
a person or period, but they could not make the
dry bones live. Guedalla is as careful a scholar,
as patient and conscientious in research and returns
from dredging in every available quarter loaded with
as rich a lumber of learning, but he can carry it
lightly, and instead of sorting it out and dumping
it down, orderly but dead, in his pages, he distils
the essence of it in the alembic of his mind, imaginatively recreates it and, like Macaulay, not only
makes the dry bones live but puts flesh on them,
restores their human attributes to them, and the
colour and warmth and movement that were theirs
when they lived.

" To-day, the writing of history," he once said
in a lecture on that subject, " is regarded with a
vague disrespect." Middle-aged men, he thought

were inclined to leave it to their elders, who were usually specialists obsessed by worship of " the original document ", and as a result history is not much read, except by reviewers and candidates for examinations. Original documents are the indispensable raw material, but unless they are worked upon by the constructive imagination of a writer they never become living history for the reader. Between 1780 and 1870 history was, said Guedalla, not only written but read; Gibbon, Macaulay and Froude were best sellers; but since then, with few exceptions, historians have suffered from an acute indigestion of facts, and history has become unreadable. I believe that was so, but the coming of Strachey, Guedalla and Emil Ludwig is bringing back the golden age of Macaulay, and intelligent readers in pursuit of pleasure are going after history again.

But Guedalla is a sort of secular trinity and, in addition to being a barrister and a historian he is a well-equipped and active politician. A year before " The Second Empire " appeared he published " The Industrial Future ", outlining a Liberal policy for reforms in industry, and while " The Second Empire " was issuing from the press he was putting up for election into Parliament as candidate for North Hackney. In 1923 and 1924 he contested North-East Derbyshire, but in the interval did a far far better thing and, in 1923, gave us another collection of his essays, " Masters and Men ", which has recently been reissued as four small volumes in the People's Library series. These essays are on all manner of topics, from Mr. Saintsbury's taste in wines to Mr. Chesterton's views on Zionism; from dissertations on Dean Inge and the poetry of Disraeli to sketches of Pitt and Mirabeau; from a caustic criticism of literary critics to an analysis of various types, English and foreign—a little perverse and trivial now and then, perhaps, but with so much of truth and sound judgment in their whimsical irony, humour and satire that they are never less than capital reading.

" A Gallery " is another of a similar kind but not so miscellaneous—a series of studies in a number of literary and political personalities, mostly contemporary, all done with such deftness of characterisation and such sagacious or cynical airiness of comment that you are not disposed to quarrel even with the author's most provocative opinions or do anything but enjoy them.

There is a further series of portrait studies in " Independence Day " (1926), but the thing is more homogeneous, for the portraits are all of kings, politicians and soldiers of England, America and France who were prominent in the American revolution, and a history of the revolution naturally grows into and out of these twelve brilliantly incisive biographies. In these Guedalla is neither hero-worshipper nor iconoclast; you get an indication of his standpoint as historian, here and in general, from a prefatory " Short Treatise on Truth ":

"One may conceivably worship, but one can never admire a god. The adored object is removed into a sphere beyond the reach of mere affection, where his appetites are starved upon a perpetually unsatisfying diet of perfunctory incense. Yet these men were once alive. Those chilly figures, in their marble attitudes, had wives and doubts and failings. . . . And there is another side to it all. Every religion breeds its sceptics. Canonisation creates the agnostic; and great names, which might have earned respect on the human plane, become the targets for young unbelievers. Nothing is more distressing than to observe the disproportionate fall which follows over-valuation. One has seen it in innumerable poets. The popular painter waits for posterity, as for a hangman. And the same monotonous pendulum, which swings national heroes to the skies, will one day drop them almost out of sight. . . . There is a stupid alternation of praise and blame; little men run about among the national images looking for feet of clay, or laboriously bleaching historical black sheep. It is a singularly aimless process; and there is no corrective, except the substitution of a clear-eyed estimate for the ecstasies of patriotic religion."

You get that clear-eyed estimate in " Independence Day ", and Washington emerges from it shorn of none of his greatness, but humanised:

"The father of his country has been deprived of his identity by his grateful children. A worse father might, perhaps, have been more accurately remembered. But the very faultlessness of that singular career seemed to invite the worst that pious ingenuity could do for him. He was encrusted with moral tales which equally repel belief and admiration; his noble figure was draped in the heavy folds of those Teutonic virtues which the Anglo-Saxon imagination erroneously attributes to the Romans. . . . He saved, in a military sense he made, the Revolution: and its happy heirs have repaid him with a withered nosegay of school-girl virtues. Misconceived panegyric has made him almost ridiculous. . . . But the General was not a Roman. Perhaps no man was ever Roman except on his monument. . . . At his burial there were three volleys and a salvo of guns. But, with an informality that must seem curious in such a case, he never lay in state. The omission has been abundantly repaired; and it is his tragedy that his reputation has been lying in state ever since."

Washington is restored to life, and gains considerably by the process, but the same clear-eyed estimate of Lafayette leaves him deprived of his halo and conventional trappings of chivalry, and reduced to the very natural, human youth of twenty that he was, excitable, irresponsible, inexperienced, an idealist, even more eager to win glory for France than freedom for America, setting out to slay " someone else's dragon " with the vaguest notion of the rights and wrongs of the case. " The best traditions of knight-errantry were respected by his profound ignorance of the persons whom he was to rescue."

The brilliance of these studies is a solid brilliance; the wit and satirical humour and pictorial effectiveness and independent thinking in them are firmly based on those " original documents " which preserve the dead facts that he has had the insight and the art to interpret and re-vitalise. The same is to be said with even more emphasis of his " Palmerston " (1927), ranging over the crowded, turbulent field of English and European politics from the end of the eighteenth to the middle of the nineteenth century, and intimately revealing Palmerston as a great human creature, one of the astutest, bluffest, greatest, least heroic and most typical English statesmen, sportsmen and gentlemen of his era. This stands, I should say, with " The Second Empire ", as the height of Guedalla's achievement—so far. One of these days, for he is the sort of man who does what he wants to do, he will become an M.P.; then you may depend he will make history as ably as he writes it, and, with his gift for paradox, it will not be surprising if he reverses the letters and transfigures himself in due season into a P.M.

JOSEPH HERGESHEIMER

THE question of whether American novelists are neglected in England is, just now, agitating literary bosoms on both sides of the Atlantic. George Jean Nathan is emphatically of opinion that English editors and reviewers systematically ignore American books; H. L. Mencken, I believe, agrees with him; and some American critics go so far as to say there is a "silent conspiracy" among our reviewers and editors for the suppression in this country of American authors and all their works. There is as little foundation for these statements as there is for the wildly melodramatic lives that are lived by terrible people in the most impossible film plays. Arnold Bennett has rightly ridiculed this morbid imagination, which sees a conspiracy where none exists, for you can satisfy yourself by merely going about with your eyes open that the American novel gets its full share of reviewing here and of popularity.

To say nothing of the great poets, essayists, humorists, novelists, philosophers of America's past, and to limit ourselves to the novelists she has produced within living memory—we did not fail to appreciate Stephen Crane, Frank Norris, Ambrose Bierce, Richard Harding Davis, Owen Wister, Winston Churchill, Mary Wilkins, Kate Douglas Wiggin, O. Henry, Alice Hegan Rice, Booth Tarkington, Robert Chambers, Mary Johnston, Zona Gale; John Russell's "Where the Pavement Ends" was a best-seller over here before it was a ditto in America, and nobody here complains that our reviewers and our public have been preoccupied with the stirring Wild West novels of dozens of American authors while the good but quieter home-made article has been left neglected in the shadow of that enthusiasm for picturesque romance. At the moment, how many English novelists receive more attention or are more popular in England than Sinclair Lewis? We were rather slow in rising to his "Main Street", but his own folk were none too quick about it; and he conquered us so completely with "Babbit" and "Martin Arrowsmith" that though he shocked our religious circles with "Elmer Gantry" we soon got over it and, at this writing, we are admiringly sitting at his feet while he analyses our national character once a week in the *Evening Standard*. Years ago, when he first came to us, we were somewhat shy of Theodore Dreiser; so they were in America; but I think we are atoning for it now by a whole-hearted recognition of his sombre realistic genius. If ever there was a conspiracy of silence it broke up with a loud noise at the touch of Edna Ferber's "So Big" and "Show Boat", at the terrible truthfulness and poignant beauty of Fanny Hurst's "Lummox" and "Appassionata", and the tender humanity and delicate art of some of the stories in her "Song of Life". We rejoice in the whimsical humour and fantasy of Christopher Morley, and the Rabelaisian allegory, irony, and Gallic wit of James Branch Cabell; and we cherish a steadily increasing appreciation of the high gifts of Sherwood Anderson. I think, then, all things considered, we ought to be acquitted of this charge of neglecting America's novelists, and might, perhaps, be told we could leave the court, if not with haloes, without a stain upon our characters, if it were not that although we have read and praised the work of Joseph Hergesheimer almost as satisfactorily as we have read and praised that of most of the novelists I have mentioned, I have a notion that he has not even yet had his full allowance here either of praise or of readers.

Born in 1880, Hergesheimer traces his descent from a Dutch family of aristocratic traditions; he attended a Quaker School in Philadelphia, and studied for a while in the Pennsylvania Academy of Fine Arts. So far as I can gather, his early years did not take him over the rough road that leads through the literary Grub Street, and I don't know whether he ever painted pictures after leaving the

Academy, but he has the sensuousness of the artist, paints pictures in his books with the artist's sensitiveness to light and shade and atmosphere, to beauty of form and colour, to the gracious charm of old houses and ordered gardens, no less than to the rich loveliness and subtly debauching miasmas of tropical places. There is this instinct for beauty, too, in the natural ease and quiet strength of his style, a style that flows lightly, urbanely through pleasant or unexciting stages of his narrative but quickens to an intensity of vividness and power in describing some scene of violence or terror, of pity or of passion.

He is as realistic as Dreiser at times, but with a difference. His realism has not the harsh, black and white solidity of Dreiser's; there is more of a feeling for romance running through it, a sort of sense of poetry that finds some mitigation of circumstance in the worst extreme. His Brandler in "Tampico" is almost as sex-obsessed as Dreiser's Cowperwood in "The Titan"; but Brandler, with all his energy and unscrupulousness, is a hesitant, vulnerable creature; his debaucheries are the ordinary squalid affairs that appeal to his kind, and he remains to the last an unclean but recognisably human being. Cowperwood goes beyond all limits and transcends humanity; he triumphs amazingly by intrigue and chicanery in vast financial deals, and occupies his intervals by defiling (I am not saying this prudishly; it is Dreiser's word) the wives and daughters of his friends and of every one in succession of a large number of women who take his fancy and, without exception, succumb to his masterful will, till he seems to your apprehension no longer human but a monstrosity, a mere super-animal. It is unbelievable that Chicago, where they are still pretty free with revolvers, would have tolerated such a universal domestic nuisance as Cowperwood, or that he could have carried through such a multitude of illicit amours without ever being embarrassed (though he lived in the '70's, before the practice of birth control) by any but the two children who were lawfully born to his first wife. Dreiser is a great and a powerful realist; he is that in the first half of Cowperwood's story, "The Financier", but in the second half, "The Titan", he goes beyond reality, builds up with amazing skill and plausibility a dehumanised monster and becomes as unconscionably but not so fantastically romantic as Dickens was when he created Quilp.

Hergesheimer's first book, "The Lay Anthony" (1914) would not, as one of his critics says, please his Presbyterian grandfather; a too-exacting standard; but even that could not be said of "Mountain Blood" (1915), nor of "Three Black Pennys", which in 1917 established his reputation. This is a story—or, rather, three stories—of three

87

generations of the Penny family, who, as one of
them tells, "some hundreds of years back acquired
a strong Welsh strain. I take it you are familiar with
the Welsh—a solitary-living, dark lot". The Pennys
are prosperous ironmasters, and the chronicle begins
with Howat Penny in eighteenth century America;
the second is the story of Jasper Penny, in the early
half, and the third of another Howat Penny, in the
latter half of the nineteenth century. It is a study
in heredity, subtly and fastidiously written, with that
imaginative cunning in reconstructing the life and
manners of bygone times, that feeling for the power
of the past over the present and love of tradition
which are influences in other of Hergesheimer's
books, and no doubt influenced himself when he
was led to adopt and adapt as his home that ancient
dwelling he describes so glamorously in "From an
Old House" (1925).

This feeling for the past is in the contrast between
the traditional breeding and pride of America's old
aristocracy and her rugged Puritan stock which
enters into one of the three stories collected in
"Gold and Iron" (1918); and there is something of
it again in "Java Head", whose scenes are laid in
old Salem town, on Massachusetts Bay, in the early
years of last century. In the breezy blusterous
Captain Jeremy Ammidon the old order is stubbornly passing, and in his hard, formal, business-

like eldest son, William, the new order is taking control; when the old man's opposition to new methods cannot otherwise be overcome, the son quietly but resolutely introduces modern improvements into their shipping business without his knowledge. But this conflict is only a trouble in the atmosphere and background of a story whose chief concern is with old Captain Jeremy's younger son, Gerrit.

In the first two chapters you are made intimate with the different members of the Ammidon family and the everyday life of their household: with Captain Jeremy, his son William, and William's wife, Rhoda, the most beautifully womanly woman I remember in any of Hergesheimer's stories. Their two elder children are normal, natural girls, and without the slightest exaggeration of sentiment the little eleven-year-old Laurel is intensely alive with all the quaintness and charm of childhood. Gerrit is absent on a voyage, and his father in particular is in a state of suppressed anxiety because his ship is several months overdue, but you get illuminating glimpses of him. Before sailing, Gerrit had been paying diffident attentions to Nettie, the illegitimate grand-daughter of the grimly puritanical old Captain Barzil Dunsack, but Dunsack had never forgiven his daughter, Kate, nor the man, Vollar, who would have married her if an untimely death had not intervened, and to avoid the further shame of his grand-daughter proving equally frail he had sternly ordered Gerrit out of his house, and Gerrit had gone to sea smarting under that rejection. The two old Captains had been good friends when both were young enough to be active master-mariners, but they had quarrelled, and hearing Dunsack was ill Captain Jeremy resolved to call and be reconciled to him. After some disjointed talk, Jeremy spoke of Gerrit's ship being long overdue and perhaps lost:

"A spasm of suffering, instantly controlled, passed over Barzil's face. 'Gerrit called once and again before he last sailed for Montevidio,' he finally pronounced. 'I stopped it and he left in a temper. I—I won't have another mortal sin here like Kate's.'

"Do you mean that Gerrit's loose?' Jeremy hotly demanded, rising. 'A more honourable boy never breathed.' Barzil was cold. 'I told him not to come back,' he repeated; 'it would only lead to—to shamefulness.' Jeremy shook his cane toward the bed. 'I may be a scoffer,' he cried, 'but I wouldn't hold a judgment over a child of mine! I'm not so damned holy that I can look down on a misfortunate girl. If Gerrit did come to see Nettie and the boy had a liking for her, why you drove away a cursed good husband. And if you think for a minute I wouldn't welcome her because that Voller fell off a yard before he could find a preacher you're an old fool!' "

The interview grew stormier; there was no reconciliation; and outside, "in the soft glow of beginning dusk, Jeremy blamed himself bitterly for his anger at the sick man". Even the chilly, formal William recognises his brother's fine qualities, and, talking of him to Rhoda, anxious about his long absence, says, "It's easy to like Gerrit; his opinions are a little wild, and an exaggerated sense of justice gets him into absurd situations; yet his motives are the purest possible. Perhaps that word pure describes him better than any other, however people who didn't know might smile. As a man, Rhoda, I can assert that he is surprisingly clean-hearted."

There is consternation in the Ammidon circle when Gerrit, at length, returns, safe and well, but with a beautiful aristocratic Chinese lady, "a Manchu and the daughter of a noble", as his wife. A like-mindedness that kept them spiritually aloof from whatever was dishonourable and dishonouring in the ways of the world had drawn those two together. Their fine loyalty to each other; her grace, dignity and gentleness; her reception by the tactful, warm-hearted Rhoda, and the rest of the family; the sensation she causes in Salem society; that tense scene when she is alone with the degenerate, opium-sodden Edward Dunsack, and proves that Gerrit had rightly realized "that her paint and embroidery covered a spirit as cold and tempered as fine metal"; and that later terrible scene when she escapes from Edward's pursuit into a bizarrely tragic death—these things and every homelier aspect of the story are worked

91

into a many-coloured, strangely patterned but harmonious whole and given an air of convincing reality.

There is a reasonable supply of averagely and even more than averagely lecherous human beings moving about in Hergesheimer's novels as there is outside them; but he has not the usual limitations of the realist: he knows that decent persons with a sense of moral responsibility, even with ideals, still exist, and that these are as real as the others. Gerrit is one such, and, in "Linda Condon" (1920) Linda is another, the staid Arnaud Hallet, whom she married, and the big, forceful, Bohemian sculptor, Dodge Pleydell, whom she loved but was afraid to marry, were others; and you might almost say that though he was probably as faulty as Pleydell, that delightful, lovable old Jew, Moses Feldt was another. The study in the growth of Linda's character—from her happy, piteous childhood, through the reaction from the life her mother is living, when she is old enough to understand it, and the spiritual and practical results of that reaction, to the gracious friendliness that grows up between Pleydell, herself and her husband, and the night when she would have left husband and children and, out of pity and love, have gone to Pleydell in the hour of his misfortune, and he, whose love has become an unselfish, disembodied thing, saves her from herself—is a beautiful and ably finished piece of work.

JOSEPH HERGESHEIMER

Charles Abbott, in "The Bright Shawl" (1922) was as clean-minded and even more of an idealist than Gerrit; he went out to Cuba, then under Spanish rule, determined, in spite of all counsel, to join the Cuban rebels in their struggle for freedom. A short book, a vividly picturesque, matter-of-fact romance, I prefer "The Bright Shawl" to its successors—"Cytherea" (1922), "Balisand", (1924), "La Calenture" (1926). In fact, I put "Three Black Pennys" and "The Bright Shawl" next in my esteem after "Java Head" and "Linda Condon", and if we are to accept Arthur Machen's dictum in "Hieroglyphics", that "ecstasy" is the quality which distinguishes "the higher from the lower in literature", then I would put "Linda Condon" where he puts "The Scarlet Letter" and "Don Quixote", among the fine things in fiction, ancient or modern.

IAN HAY

THERE has been a little excitement lately over the
the facts that H. G. Wells, Arnold Bennett, and
other distinguished novelists, have introduced living
persons into their novels under slight disguises, or
without any disguise at all. But there is nothing
new in this; it has been an old trick of the trade
since the days of Fielding and Smollett. As a rule,
such living persons have figured in fiction under
assumed names, but the change of name has seldom
served to conceal their identities. Dickens, Thackeray, Disraeli were great sinners in that way; if it is
a sin for artists to work from a model, and there
are strictly proper people who still believe that it is
and denounce it as particularly shocking. Dickens
got into trouble for caricaturing Leigh Hunt in
Harold Skimpole, and I daresay there were some
who thought it a breach of good taste on his part
to pillory as Mr. Squeers, that Yorkshire schoolmaster who threatened him with an action for libel.

But I have never been able to see why a novelist
should not take his material wherever he finds it;
why he should not use real men and women for his

characters as he uses real houses, streets, districts, for his scenery, real personal experiences, things he has heard and seen, for his dialogue and incidents. If he knows his business (and if he does not whatever he may do is of no consequence) you may depend he is no slavish copyist, but imaginatively adapts to his own purpose all the facts he makes use of, and his justification for doing so is that the novel whose characters and events have this foundation in reality is always more naturally alive than is the novel that has been constructed by its author entirely from what Lord Fopling Flutter called "the sprouts of his own imagination".

When I read the first novels of Ian Hay—or, to give him his full name, Major John Hay Beith—I had a suspicion that he was not spinning all his characters and all their stories out of airy nothing. His people are too lifelike never to have lived. You could read in and between his lines that he had been a Public School boy; was or had been a schoolmaster; had seen something of clerical life and of the political world from the inside; that he was a golfer, a cricketer, and in general a keen sportsman; that human beings he had known had sat to him for at least some of his characters; and nowadays, when I know more of his biography, I find it does not differ greatly from what his novels had led me to surmise.

IAN HAY

Born on April 17th, 1876, Major Beith is the second son of the late John Alexander Beith, and grandson of the Rev. Dr. Beith, of Stirling, who is still remembered in certain Highland parishes as one of the great figures of the Disruption of 1843. A man of remarkable zeal and energy, Major Beith's father was not contented to limit his activities to the direction of the big shipping and export business of Beith, Stevenson & Co., but devoted almost the whole of his leisure to public service. He was President of the Manchester Chamber of Commerce, Government Representative on the Mersey Dock Board, a J.P. for Lancaster, and a director and supporter of almost innumerable philanthropic and religious enterprises. In politics he was an ardent follower of Gladstone, and was for some time leader of the Liberal Party in Manchester. In philanthropic work he was closely associated with men of such irreconcilable political opinions as Jacob Bright and Sir W. H. Houldsworth. The little recreation he allowed himself was mostly taken aboard a boat, and his favourite holiday place was Oban, which had been his father's first parish. He purchased Alt-na-Craig, Professor Blackie's eyrie overlooking the Sound of Kenera, when the eccentric Professor indignantly vacated it on the advent of the railway.

Fettes, that home of classical scholarship and Rugby football, counts Ian Hay among its distin-

97

guished scholars. He spent his early student days there as the fag of the head-boy, J. A. Simon, now his friend the sometime Attorney-General, Sir John Simon, K.C., M.P. In 1895 he went to St. John's College, Cambridge, where he was so far from slothful that he played Rugby football three days a week, and on the remaining three laboured at the oar with such diligence that he attained ("rather flukily", he says) to the post of Captain of his College Boat Club during his last year. Incidentally, he devoted sufficient attention to his studies to obtain a Second Class in the Classical Tripos.

Thus equipped, he put it abroad that his knowledge was at the service of the Headmasters of the nation; but as nothing happened (beyond two temporary engagements at Charterhouse and Fettes) he concluded that classical degrees were a drug in the market and, returning to Cambridge, spent a laborious year in acquiring a sufficient knowledge of chemistry and physics to fit him for a Senior Mastership.

Thereafter, he became for ten years a senior master, for four at Durham School, and for six very happy years at his old school, Fettes. Then a partial breakdown in health, the result of burning the candle at both the scholastic and the literary ends, moved him regretfully to resign his post and turn his back for ever on a profession which, whatever

98

its trials and disappointments, provides its adherents, as he says, with a never-failing supply of the healthiest and most invigorating company in the world—that of the British schoolboy; and one that, incidentally, has supplied Ian Hay with material which he had, even before that resignation, turned to excellent account in his first novel. For "Pip" begins by being one of the best and most natural stories of schoolboy life and character, and in its later phases blends a love romance with great doings at cricket and golf, and blends it with them in a manner which indicates that he has done more than read and write about them.

As far back as 1901, while he was at Cambridge qualifying for that Senior Mastership, Ian Hay had begun to coquet with fiction. He had worked fitfully on a school story, the hero of which was modelled, he confesses, on a certain Fettes boy of his acquaintance. He called this boy "Pip", and what is now the third chapter in that novel was the first serious attempt he ever made at writing fiction. The tale grew in a desultory way through several years. Sometimes he did not touch it for six months at a stretch; sometimes he took it up again and interpolated a chapter into its hero's past; sometimes he grafted an episode on to his future. The school scenes were done first; then the love scenes; then the first two chapters which are concerned with

99

LIBRARY

OKALOOSA-WALTON JUNIOR COLLEGE

the somewhat neglected home-life of Pip and his sister, Pipette, and give an amusing record of their experiences at the local kindergarten school kept by Mr., Miss Mary, Miss Arabella and Miss Amelia Pocklington. Among the good things in this and all Ian Hay's novels are his humorous and reflective asides, such as those in "Pip" on the fascination of golf; on how a schoolmaster realises early in his career that "he is not a universally popular person"; or on how Pip's father, a widower, discovers he has not acted wisely in leaving his two children under the influence of the servants, for it has come to pass that etiquette and deportment are summed up for Pip and Pipette "in the following nursery laws, as amended by the kitchen":—

"1. Girls, owing to some mysterious infirmity which is never apparent, and for which they are not responsible, must be helped first to everything.

"2. A boy must on no account punch a girl, even though she is older and bigger than himself. (For reason see 1.)

"3. A girl must not scratch a boy. (Not that the boy matters, but it is unladylike.)

"4. Real men do not play with dolls. (However, you may pretend to be a doctor and administer medicine without loss of dignity.)

"5. Real ladies do not climb the trees in the garden in the Square. (But you can get over the difficulty by pretending to be a boy or a monkey for half an hour.)

"6. Girls never have dirty hands—only boys. (For solution of this difficulty see note on 5.)

"7. You must *never* tell tales. Girls must be specially careful about this, not because they are more prone to do so, but because boys think they are.

"8. Real men never kiss girls, but they may sometimes permit girls to kiss them.

"9. You must eat up your bread and butter before you have any cake. (This rule holds good, they found out later, all through life.)

"10. Do not blow upon your tea to cool it; this is very vulgar. Pour it into your saucer instead."

Having an uneasy suspicion that, as the story progressed, he was making Pip too much of a bread-and-butter hero, the author sternly deprived him of all his money and sent him out to earn his living as a chauffeur; then, as a last straw, he invented a mildly lurid episode which he labelled "The Principal Boy: An Interlude", and dovetailed this into the narrative immediately before Pip's final apotheosis; and by this time, he says, "the original Pip had faded almost entirely from the scheme of things. It nearly always happens that when one sets out to include a 'real live' person in a 'made-up' story the exigencies of the narrative make it necessary to develop the character in some unexpected direction. Hence the stolid, immovable features of my original Pip were stretched and strained to a quite unrecognisable degree. But in spite of the liberties which I have taken with his character and (probably) with his history, I still have to thank my Fettes friend for supplying me with the original materials—his devotion to cricket, his entire lack of imagination, and his freakish memory—for my story."

Early in 1907, looking over what he had done, Ian Hay realised that he had written a book. So he had it typed and dispatched it on a short journey of a mile or so to the offices of the historic house of Blackwood, in Edinburgh. Within six weeks it was accepted, and that autumn it was published. Anxious not to hurt the susceptibilities of his sensitive profession (for he was then a master at Fettes) the author cut off the last third of his name and "Pip" appeared with the now familiar "Ian Hay" on its title page. It was very favourably received, was soon in a second edition, and has gone on selling and growing in popularity to this day.

"Pip" is only Ian Hay's first book so far as the public is concerned. Two years earlier he had issued a small, privately printed volume of University sketches, which is not to be had, nowadays, for love or money, but he owns that more than once he has employed small portions of it "to season later dishes." Even so, his beginnings are in "Pip", since he wrote that first chapter of it which is now the third as long ago as 1901.

In the spring of 1908 Blackwood suggested that he should follow up the successful "Pip" with another book that autumn, and though it had taken him six years to write his first book, he wrote his second, "The Right Stuff", in six months, and by October it was scoring a new success. His third, "A Man's Man," ran serially in *Blackwood's* before it appeared between covers. The heroes of "The Right Stuff" and "A Man's Man" unlike each other in almost every other respect, have this in common—that each *is* a man's man. It is a type that particularly appeals to Ian Hay, though he knows and depicts a variety of other types with equal insight, and his gallery of women characters is a full and varied one. "A Safety Match" followed in 1911, and ten years later he dramatised this and won his second success on the stage with it, having won his first with the delightful "Tilly of Bloomsbury" in 1919.

"Happy-go-Lucky" and "A Knight on Wheels" had added to his popularity as a novelist when the war came, and he went on active service. The war years produced that poignantly humorous and pathetic story of Kitchener's Army, "The First

Hundred Thousand", and its complement, "The Last Million". In 1926 he visited Gallipoli and Salonica and told the story of that pilgrimage in "The Ship of Remembrance". But with the return of peace he had returned to his proper calling and in "The Willing Horse" (1921) "The Lucky Number", "Paid With Thanks", "Half a Sovereign", and the rest of his recent novels, you find that his hand has lost none of its cunning, his humour none of its spontaneity, his sympathy with human weaknesses and his belief in the general decency and goodness of average men and women none of their charm and breadth of understanding. He handles that amiable, butterfly creature, the "freak", in "Happy-go-Lucky", whimsically, satirically, but as Izaak Walton said the angler should handle the worm he puts on his hook, as if he loved him, and it is characteristic of his genial philosophy that he shows how this drifting, weak-willed, aimless philanderer, because he has the right stuff in him, is completely transformed when he is taken in hand by the right girl. Within their range, his characters are, in a day when so many turn the novel into a primer on sex-psychology, true to life and alive; above all, Ian Hay is a teller of tales about the sort of people we know; and he knows how to tell them —that is why he has such a multitude of readers.

ROBERT HICHENS

THERE is a tradition that every novelist began as a writer of verse, and if Robert Hichens did not exactly conform to it, he did not altogether break with it, for in his youth he wrote both verse and prose, but without regarding either as the business of his life. His first absorbing ambition was to become a musician; he sacrificed a career at Oxford to this end, and, leaving Clifton College, studied music for some years at Bristol and at the Royal College, in London. His instruments were the piano and the organ, and he acquired a considerable mastery of them. He never made his début professionally, but played several times in public at charity concerts with success that was satisfying enough; but he was not one of those who mistake the desire to achieve for the power to achieve; he always had a healthy instinct for looking facts in the face, a long-sighted faculty of self-criticism; and he was not slow to realise that however hard he might practise he would never be able to make a great musician of himself; and as soon as he felt sure of this he abandoned the attempt to do so.

THE GLORY THAT WAS GRUB STREET

Through all that experimental period he had been writing tales, essays, recitations, and scores of lyrics for music; his lyrics alone in one year brought him in over a hundred pounds. One of the first lyrics he sold, "If at Your Window", was set to music by Ethel Harraden, sister of Beatrice Harraden, the novelist; another, "A Kiss and Good-Bye", was set by Tito Mattei and sung by Madame Patti at the Albert Hall.

"In the natural pride of my heart," Robert Hichens confessed to me when we were talking of this some while ago, "I took a seat in the stalls and waited in a fever of anxiety to hear how it would come off. It was received with such enthusiastic applause that I was lifted into a heaven of delight, but as Madame Patti returned, in response to insistent cries of 'Encore!' I was tumbled headlong down out of my heaven by hearing two voices from the seats just behind me: 'What a lovely song that was!' one exclaimed rapturously. 'Yes,' the other grudgingly agreed, 'but what awful rot the words of these songs always are!'"

Born in 1864, Robert Hichens was the eldest son of Canon Hichens, Rector of St. Stephen's, near Canterbury. He was about twenty-four when he decided that there was no future for him as a musician and began to feel his way toward a different goal. So far, he had been writing stories mainly for his own amusement; he had also written two long novels which he had never dreamt of publishing; but a third, written when he was seventeen, "The Coastguard's Secret", he offered to a publisher, and was so impressed when that publisher said he was willing to risk half the cost of publishing it that he risked the other half himself and his book appeared, and was not unkindly received by the reviewers.

But it languished, and died, and has long been out of print. I could not lead Hichens to tell me more of it than that it was a kind of ghost story—a very bad one—merely the crude sort of thing you would expect from a youngster still in his 'teens. When, after the brilliant success of "The Green Carnation", the publisher of "The Coastguard's Secret" urged that the time was ripe to put out a new edition of it, its author was filled with direst alarm and by prayer and protest dissuaded him from his purpose.

Seeking the best way to his new goal, while that now unobtainable novel was still the only one to his name, Hichens became a pupil at the late David Anderson's School of Journalism; shortly before he joined, Francis Gribble had left it, and among his fellow-pupils were Bernard Hamilton, Guy Berringer and Cranstoun Metcalfe.

I gathered from Robert Hichens that he had endowed Felix, in his novel of that name, with certain of his own characteristics and some of his own autobiography. And if you turn to "Felix" you will find there delightfully amusing descriptions of Sam Carringbridge and his School of Journalism in the Strand which tally closely enough with what Hichens told me of his experiences with David Anderson. At a loose end in London, Felix, then only one-and-twenty, meets Hugo Arliss, learns that Arliss is "a sucking Kipling" studying at Sam's School, and eagerly accepts the offer of an introduction to that institution. He calls, and being summoned into Mr. Carringbridge's presence, finds him a large, handsome, urbane personage, beautifully dressed and smoking a cigar:

"Mr. Hugo Arliss told me about your school," Felix began, in an unusually low voice and feeling soothed almost as if by a narcotic.

"Mr. Arliss, a charming, intelligent, gentlemanly fellow. I am very much attached to him," said Mr. Carringbridge. . . .

"I met him in France," said Felix. . . . "Arliss advised me to see if I could enter at your school for a year. I am very keen on trying to write."

"It is a great profession. The journalist is a power. . . . You know my terms?"

Felix jumped—the last sentence came with such a mellifluous abruptness from Mr. Carringbridge's bright red lips.

"No. Arliss didn't——"

"Dear careless fellow. One hundred guineas payable to me on the day I sign the agreement. You merely hand me your cheque and I bind myself forthwith to give you

the advantage—if it be one, possibly not!—of my personal
teaching and experience for one whole year, and to allow
you the free and unfettered use of the writing-hall you
have just passed through. I also give you ink——"

A generous smile illumined his face.

"It's awfully good of you," Felix had murmured, before
he knew that he was going to murmur anything.

"But not pens and paper. I find young men prefer to
consult their personal taste in those matters, and therefore
I give them free scope. About ink there is less divergence
of opinion, and mine, I believe, gives general satisfaction.
I am glad if it is so. I never drive the young."

"No?" said Felix.

"Never. I lead them, perhaps. I show them what a
man can do, has done. You see the volumes on that
table? . . . Those contain the leading articles written by
me for the *Daily Recorder* during twenty-five years of active
journalistic life. My pupils can read them at any time."

"You must have worked tremendously hard," said
Felix, counting the volumes.

There were eight of them, and they were tremendously
fat. He felt almost awe-stricken. Mr. Carringbridge
indulged himself and Felix in a lotus-eating smile.

"I have been through the mill," he replied lazily. . . .
"If my pupils like to take me as an example they would
do well to follow," he continued, "they can. I come up
from Brighton every day by the nine o'clock train. But
I never drive them. I trust them. I rely on them. I
give them complete liberty. When do you propose to
come?"

At the end of his term, Felix was assured by
Carringbridge that he would certainly get on; not
perhaps as a journalist, but he had detected greater
than journalistic gifts in him and urged him to
develop these. It is more than likely that, at the

end of his term at David Anderson's School, Anderson gave Hichens similar advice. Anyhow, at Anderson's Hichens worked hard, writing all manner of descriptive and leading articles and submitting them to him, and at the same time he was sending manuscripts to the magazines and newspapers, having many rejected and a steadily increasing proportion accepted. About this date and in the few succeeding years, he contributed articles to the *European Mail* and the *Evening Standard* and, like so many authors who have since become famous, supplied his quota of "turnovers" to the late lamented *Globe*. But he was not destined to be a journalist, even though for a time he did musical and dramatic notes for *Hearth and Home*, the *Gentlewoman* and various other papers, and succeeded Bernard Shaw as musical critic of the *World*.

Returning in those early years from a holiday in Egypt, Hichens wrote a story, "The Collaborators", and sent it to the *Pall Mall Magazine*. The editor, Sir Douglas Straight, promptly accepted it, and asked for more, and more were sent and taken. When, in 1894, Hichens offered him "The Green Carnation", Sir Douglas saw it was quite unsuitable for a magazine serial but, recognising its brilliance, forwarded it with a strong recommendation to Heinemann, the publisher. The success of "The Green Carnation"—which, apart from the boyish

SINCLAIR LEWIS.

ROBERT HICHENS

"Coastguard's Secret", was Hichens's first book, was immediate and immense. As everyone knows, it satirised Oscar Wilde and the æsthetic movement, then in full blast. It was written without the least touch of malice, and merely because the subject was ready to hand. Hichens only knew Wilde causally; had met him no more than four times before he wrote the book, and never met him after; and so far as he heard Wilde took it all in good part and with characteristic imperturbability.

Curiously enough, though it came out while "The Green Carnation" was still the sensation of the day, "An Imaginative Man" met with but moderate success, and a year later "The Folly of Eustace" was scarcely more fortunate. "Flames" (1897), that finely imaginative, haunting, spiritualistic romance, had a more stirring reception, and after discussing it at large in the *Review of Reviews*, W. T. Stead gave us a tabloid edition of it for a penny; nevertheless, it fell short of the triumph of "The Green Carnation". Hichens's seven books of the next seven years were acclaimed by the critics but their sales were not extraordinary, yet they included "The Londoners", "Felix", and so poignant and masterly a story as "The Woman with the Fan". In the year after "The Woman with the Fan", however (1905), appeared "The Garden of Allah", and then the reading world hesitated no longer. Within three months that greatest of Hichens's novels had run through five editions, and how many it has gone through since I would not say at a venture. Of his fourteen more recent novels—"Barbary Sheep", "The Call of the Blood", "Bella Donna", down to "The God Within Him" (1926)—able and popular as they are, none has reached the high literary and imaginative qualities or the popularity of "The Garden of Allah".

He has felt the lure of the stage, and among plays of his that have been produced are "Daughters of Babylon", in collaboration with Wilson Barrett; "The Medicine Man", with H. D. Traill, in which Irving played the principal part; "Becky Sharp", "The Real Woman", "The Voice from the Minaret", but the dramatic power and long success of "The Garden of Allah", which he dramatised in 1920, has eclipsed them all.

For long past Hichens has had no settled home in this country. He came to London in 1884, when he was twenty, and lived here for fifteen years. Then a troublesome illness affected his nerves, and finding the endless noise and hurry and excitement of the town unendurable, he went abroad to look for the seclusion and quiet that were necessary to him. He became very much of a dweller in hotels, with a pleasant place where he could work at peace

in Sicily. He laughs at the notion of a novelist
roaming the earth in search of human material or
local colour. Living in Sicily, he came to know its
atmosphere, its spirit, its people, and was moved
to write about them as spontaneously as he was
moved to write of London while he lived here.
"Felix" and "The Londoners" are not more
essentially born of London than "The Call of the
Blood" is of Sicily, or "The Garden of Allah" more
essentially inspired by the magic and glamour and
mystery of the desert. His stories grow in his mind
out of whatever life happens to be round about
him. He had no thought of writing anything
about the Sahara until he had been there many
times, but by degrees the strange spell of it laid
hold upon him, and it was not until after a seventh
sojourn in the desert that he was moved to begin
writing "The Garden of Allah".

On one of those seven occasions, he visited a
Trappist monastery and, drawn by its air of perfect
restfulness, said he wished he could stay there for
a while. "We take guests," remarked the lay
brother who was showing him round. "We should
be glad to have you if you do not mind living very
simply". For three weeks Hichens lived there
frugally, sleeping in one of the small, bare cells.
From there he went into the desert with the Arab
poet whom in the novel he has named Batouch, for

his guide, and as they stood one evening gazing across the waste of sand toward the sunset, a chance phrase of Batouch's woke in him a first vague thought of "The Garden of Allah". Talking in his usual dreamy monotone, Batouch said, "This is the garden of oblivion. In the desert one forgets everything, even the desire of one's soul". This saying somehow called a vision of the secluded, prison-like monastery back into its hearer's mind, and with it came a fancy of bringing one of the monastery's silent tenants out here into the desert and letting him forget, in this garden of oblivion, his vows, his hopes, his God, and be willing to lose even his soul for the love of a woman.

But another five years passed before the story shaped itself and he could see his way through it, and then he spent the better part of two years translating it into words, slowly and with infinite pains which were amply justified by the result. For whatever else may be lost in the desert, it was there that, as a novelist, Hichens found himself.

A. E. HOUSMAN

A. E. HOUSMAN

OCCASION took me the other day to the British Museum Reading Room and to while away the rather long interval of waiting for books to be brought to me, I took down an old volume of the Annual Register out of an idle curiosity to see what was happening in the world of letters in the year of my nativity. Thackeray was just dead, and Dickens, the chronicler informed me, was issuing "Our Mutual Friend", and Trollope "The Small House at Allington" in monthly parts, and Reade was publishing "Hard Times" (or "Very Hard Times" as he originally called it). Miss Braddon and Mrs. Henry Wood were then the most popular women novelists. In poetry, Tennyson reigned in kingly loneliness, with Browning greatly respected but quite a small star to the moon of Tennyson's glory. It was mentioned that "Enoch Arden" had been received that year with immense enthusiasm, and, the recorder added, such was its vogue that it was not easy to go into a drawing-room where you would not find a copy of "Enoch Arden" lying on the table, and if you went on a railway journey you were almost sure to notice that at least one passenger in your carriage would bring the book out of his pocket and become absorbed in reading it.

Tennyson, in fact, shared the popularity of Dickens; he was as supreme in one art as Dickens was in another; but we have no poet nowadays who so towers above his fellows, none who has so subdued the public with his magic that the reading world, roused to excitement by the news that he has finished a new book, hurries out in thousands to spend money in buying it as soon as it is printed. This does not happen now; none of our poets has been able to take such miraculous hold on a vast multitude either by the power of his verse or the picturesque charm of his personality. There are several reasons for this. For one thing all our poets now cut their hair short, are clean shaven, dress like stockbrokers or city clerks, and mix with the crowd as if there were no difference between them and the next man. They are no longer wrapped in mystery as a race apart, like the Levites; they look commonplace and ordinary, and this discourages the public from believing they or their works are otherwise; and the portraits of them scattered freely through the press give them away even to people who have not seen them. I suppose it is difficult to go hero-worshipping unless the hero either looks the part or holds impressively aloof and keeps out of sight.

A. E. HOUSMAN

Another reason for the apathy of the general reader is, perhaps, that the poetry written to-day is not so great, or does not seem so great to him as the poetry of Tennyson seemed to our grandfathers. The only poet of our time who wakened such enthusiasm that his name was in the mouths of everybody, whether they had read him or not, so that the publication of a new poem or book of poems by him became an event of national interest, was Kipling. But with the passing of years this glow of eager enthusiasm even for him has cooled and dwindled, until now the influence of his name merely warms the system of the general reader to a respectable ardour.

Probably the Victorians were more emotional, more generously impulsive, less hypercritical and sophisticated than we are; they still believed poets were inspired, but we have been so over-fed with all manner of wonders in these latter years that our poets have lost that halo, and we rank them indifferently with practitioners of other ingeniously mechanical, unsensational crafts. It is significant that one poet who was good but not popular enough to have any "news value" died recently and was ignored by all our weekly papers, their space being too much occupied with urgent accounts of distinguished burglars, eminent ladies and gentlemen with a talent for playing tennis, baby Princesses who,

strangely gifted, have succeeded in getting born of
the blood Royal, and other very important persons.
Poets, of course, could have no place in such dazzling
company.

Yet, if they cannot compete with the popularity
of these notabilities, nor with that of eloquent barristers or politicians, many of our poets do obtain
fit audiences though few and occasionally a little
money; some of them obtain audiences that are
equally fit and not few and, it may be hoped, a
little more money accordingly. One of these last
is, surprisingly enough, A. E. Housman—surprisingly, because he is one of the most original of living
poets, and adds to this disadvantage by making no
concessions to popular sentiment: he is a steady
pessimist, with no idealistic illusions about life or
love or any of those things which it is believed
poets must idealise if they wish to be taken to the
world's heart. He has no affectations, does not
attempt to startle the simple with any acrobatic
contortions in *vers libre*, but uses a simple, direct,
almost nakedly plain English, usually writing it in
the easiest, homeliest, most familiar of metres.
Moreover, he shuns publicity, lives in retirement as
a Fellow of Trinity College, Cambridge, where he
is Professor of Latin, and you seldom meet anybody
who has seen him or knows anything much about
him.

A. E. HOUSMAN

In thirty-two years he has published only two small books of poems, which have no wide variety of tone or theme, but are mostly sombre or grimly humorous, tersely realistic lyrics redolent of the fields, the villages, towns and folk of his own county, Shropshire, with two or three that are reminiscent of London where, from 1882 to 1892, he worked as a higher division clerk in the Patent Office. He was in London when he wrote, for instance, of the statue he met in the Grecian gallery which, as it steadfastly looked at him—

> "Well met," I thought the look would say,
> "We both were fashioned far away;
> We neither knew, when we were young,
> These Londoners we live among."

And from this and the other London poems you visualise him as a lonely figure never feeling at home in the great city or much in sympathy with its alien people:

> "In my own shire, if I was sad,
> Homely comforters I had. . . .
> But here in London streets I ken
> No such helpmates, only men;
> And these are not in plight to bear,
> If they would, another's care.
> They have enough as 'tis; I see
> In many an eye that measures me
> The mortal sickness of a mind
> Too unhappy to be kind."

119

THE GLORY THAT WAS GRUB STREET

"The Shropshire Lad" made its appearance in 1896, and in the next eleven years it went through eight editions. Then, in 1907, it was issued in a charmingly neat little edition, so small it will fit into a waistcoat pocket, and sold, if I remember rightly (for I bought it) at sixpence. It is still to be had, but its post-war price has risen to eighteen pence; and how many thousands it has sold at that lower and higher price, before the war and after, is more than I can say. But I know that when I was on a visit to the front in France and Belgium, during the war, the three volumes of verse that were greatly in demand among the soldiers of the new Army, down at the rest camps, were Browning's "Men and Women", Omar Khayyâm, and that excellent pocket edition of "The Shropshire Lad".

It is not so curious as it may seem at first blush that "The Shropshire Lad", with its philosophically pessimistic outlook, should appeal to those men who had been in the firing line and were shortly going up again. For what is loosely called its pessimism is not so much that as a courageously stoical acceptance of the stern facts of human experience. The soldier who could find any pleasure at all in verse was in no mood, just then, for gracious sentiment or optimistic fancies; he was up against stark realities; accustomed to the sight of death and the thought of its immanence, had shed nearly all his illusions, found a fearful and perhaps morbid joy in treating such things as a grim jest, and the honest facing of the truth in "The Shropshire Lad", its wry, whimsical, indomitable realism, must have chimed with his own thoughts and strengthened him to endure the fate that is, in the long run, common to all men.

He would read songs of the soldier going off to earlier wars, but they are not charged with heartening rhetoric of victory and glory awaiting him; they are songs touched with the emotion and irony of bare truthfulness, such as that on the Queen's jubilee, when the bonfires blaze on the hills,

> "Because 'tis fifty years to-night
>   That God has saved the Queen.
>
> Now, when the flame they watch not towers
>   About the soil they trod,
> Lads, we'll remember friends of ours
>   Who shared the work with God.
>
> To skies that knit their heartstrings right,
>   To fields that bred them brave,
> The saviours come not home to-night:
>   Themselves they could not save. . . .
>
> Oh, God will save her, fear you not:
>   Be you the men you've been,
> Get you the sons your fathers got,
>   And God will save the Queen."

That is the key-note of Housman's half-dozen songs of soldiering, and there is something finer,

more inspiriting in it than in any glamour or romantic
sentiment, as there is in that magnificently robust
"Epitaph on an Army of Mercenaries", which is
included in "Last Poems" (1922) and turns the
sordid truth into a crown of glory for the "Old
Contemptibles", who "took their wages and are
dead":

> "Their shoulders held the sky suspended;
>   They stood, and earth's foundations stay;
> What God abandoned, these defended,
>   And saved the sum of things for pay."

The difference between Wordsworth and Housman
is that Wordsworth is, even when he lapses into
paganism, conscious of a spiritual significance underlying the life of nature and of man; and Housman
is a realist preoccupied with things seen, and often
obsessed by a sense of their futility.   The blackbird,
in "The Shropshire Lad", sings:

> "Lie down, lie down, young yeoman;
>   What use to rise and rise?
> Rise man a thousand mornings
>   Yet down at last he lies,
>   And then the man is wise."

And "Last Poems" echoes this feeling of the use-
lessness of it all in the song of getting up, washing,
dressing, eating, drinking and working "God knows
why":

A. E. HOUSMAN

"Oh, often have I washed and dressed,
    And what's to show for all my pain?
Let me lie abed and rest:
Ten thousand times I've done my best,
    And all's to do again."

Always the verses are haunted by the thought of
death and change, or the frailty of love and friendship, as in that often quoted dialogue between the
dead and buried man and his living friend, with its
bizarre close:

"Is my friend hearty,
    Now I am thin and pine,
And has he found to sleep in
    A better bed than mine?

Yes, lad, I lie easy,
    I lie as lads would choose;
I cheer a dead man's sweetheart,
    Never ask me whose."

This is the burden of more than one poem, and
again and again these lyrics are a brief psalm of
life whose goal is the grave, and Housman makes
his apologia for this in the lines where a friend
reproaches him with,

"Pretty friendship 'tis to rhyme
Your friends to death before their time,"

and he replies:

"Oh many a peer of England brews
Livelier liquor than the Muse,
And malt does more than Milton can
To justify God's ways to man.

123

THE GLORY THAT WAS GRUB STREET

Ale, man, ale's the stuff to drink
For fellows whom it hurts to think;
Look into the pewter pot
To see the world as the world's not. . . .

Therefore, since the world has still
Much good, but much less good than ill,
And while the sun and moon endure
Luck's a chance, but trouble's sure,
I'd face it as a wise man would,
And train for ill and not for good."

In a prefatory paragraph in his "Last Poems" Housman says it is unlikely that he will write many more, and closes the volume with "Fancy's Knell", which ends on a note that is very characteristic of his Muse:

"To-morrow, more's the pity,
Away we both must hie,
To air the ditty,
And to the earth I."

But there are a hundred and four "ditties" in these two small books of his, and their last to-morrow is farther off than ours, for they are not so mortal as are those Shropshire loves and lives whose mortality inspired nearly all of them.

VIOLET HUNT

It is customary to speak of the artistic temperament as if it had been reduced to a standard
pattern—as if it invariably manifested itself in one and
the same fashion. This careless attempt to stereo-
type what is really a most protean spirit has been
responsible for misleading many young men who are
not artists into adopting the particular (and not
always too particular) habits, idiosyncrasies, eccentricities supposed to denote that temperament, under
the impression that their having acquired its recognised peculiarities of manner and conduct is in
itself evidence that they must also be artistic.

The artistic temperament, however, is no such
mechanical and monotonous form of self-indulgence.
It develops spontaneously in all who are artists, and
can be spuriously developed in many who are not;
and when it is the real thing it is as diverse in its
ways of asserting itself as are the infinitely varied
characters of men and women. It made Milton
austere, and Herrick more lively than beseemed one
of his cloth; accommodated itself to Byron's vices
and to Matthew Arnold's virtues; to Rossetti's

Bohemianism and Browning's respectability. It sends one artist into seclusion, another into society; makes one a misanthrope, another a lover of his kind; one a self-centred egoist, dead to all interests but his own, another a genial sentimentalist whose sympathies are ready for all who need them; it afflicts one with a ridiculous conceit of himself, and another with an almost equally ridiculous diffidence and humility.

Difference of sex makes no difference in the workings of this variable artistic temperament. I could tell of how it drives one of the truest of modern women poets to sit and write at her desk for regular hours every morning, and prompts another, who is not more gifted, to write anywhere at any time when inspiration comes to her, and sometimes prevents her from writing anything for weeks together; of how it renders a country quietness and freedom from interruption essential to the work of one accomplished woman novelist, and the stir and friendly neighbourhood and stimulation of town-life or the excitement of travel as essential to that of another.

And Violet Hunt I should guess to be one of these latter. She has for long past made her home in London, and you may frequently meet her here at literary dinners and social gatherings, or at more fashionable salons where men and women distinguished or becoming distinguished in art or

letters are wont to congregate and rub shoulders
with persons of importance in the business and
political worlds. Moreover, you learn from her
sometimes elusive, sometimes amazingly candid
autobiography, "The Flurried Years", that she
loves and has always loved good society—that is,
the society of interesting people who are doing things
in the arts, and that she was and is never happier
than when she is playing hostess at one of those
pleasant, delightfully informal salons of her own.
From time to time she has entertained in the drawing-
room of her house on Campden Hill, where Gaudier
Brjeska's startlingly futurist bust of Ezra Pound is
pedestalled in the garden, more famous authors and
artists and miscellaneous celebrities than I have
space to catalogue; and she opens her 1913 autobiographical chapter with the rapturous ejaculation,
"Home, and my yearly garden party never so well
attended. Cabinet Ministers, by Jove!" and proceeds
to chronicle briefly, "*Fêtes champetres* at the Monds'
in Lowndes Square, Henley with the Harmsworths,
the Cabaret Club with all the charming artist rabble
who were on the top of the vogue." There is a
natural exuberance in her enjoyment of these things
that reminds you rather of Charles Lamb's almost
weeping in the motley Strand for sheer joy in so
much life. She notes, immediately after the report
of this dazzling social round, that she withdrew

to the restfulness of a cottage at Selsey, but even then cannot refrain from adding, "A gorgeous season. I wished my poor mother had been there to see it." No recluse, no hater of madding crowds speaks in all this; and she is too good a conversationalist, who can on occasion administer a caustically witty sting with one of the softest of voices, and is too easily at home among crowds, either as hostess or visitor, not to have given more of her heart to society than to solitude.

Although Violet Hunt was born in the staid old cathedral city of Durham, and in the later years of that Victorian era which is now regarded as dull and prim and dowdily old-fashioned, she has a vivacious unconventionality, an independence and modernity of outlook that seem to make her more of the twentieth than of the nineteenth century. Her father was a well-known artist, her mother a novelist, and she numbered among the friends of her family Browning, Millais, Burne-Jones, Ruskin, the Rossettis—and, by the way, she has been busy for some while past on a book of her Memories of the Rossettis, which will probably have seen the light before these lines are printed.

In 1912 she completed and published a novel called "The Governess", which had been commenced and left unfinished by her mother long before; but by then she had become a well-known novelist herself. Her own first book, "The Maiden's Progress", a novel in dialogue, made its appearance in 1894; and before 1912 she had followed it with ten other novels or volumes of short stories including "The Human Interest", "A Hard Woman", "Unkist, Unkind", "Affairs of the Heart", "The Celebrity at Home", "White Rose of Weary Leaf", and in 1910 "The Wife of Altamont" and "Tales of the Uneasy". To my thinking, the best of these are "White Rose of Weary Leaf" and the brilliant collection of stories in "Tales of the Uneasy".

The tales in the earlier "Affairs of the Heart" (1900) are unequal as well as varied; they are clever, entertaining stories of *fin de siècle* London life, passionate, bizarre, humorous, but none of them remains so vividly in one's memory as does that bitterly ironic story of the girl who pretends to be a reckless decadent in the hope of pleasing a man who is as decadent as she pretends to be, only to find she has taken the wrong way to charm him and he has fallen in love with a slip of a girl who has all the innocence and simplicity she herself had affected to have lost. But "Tales of the Uneasy" show throughout a surer mastery of the short-story writer's art. Some of these tales, pleasant and unpleasant, of the occult and of real life with the gilt off, are the most brilliant things of the kind Miss Hunt has done—one, that harrowing, haunting story of the eugenist mother and her child, "The Tiger Skin", is a little masterpiece and, as a very long short story, has since been reissued in a book to itself.

"The Celebrity at Home", in a lighter vein, is the terribly candid and disrespectful record kept by his daughter of the doings of Mr. Vero-Taylor, a successful dramatist who is a tuft-hunter in high society and neglects his wife and family for the pursuit of those higher things. Much of it is capital farce, and those who coruscate in certain easy-going social circles are depicted with a quietly pungent, genially humorous satire. "White Rose of Weary Leaf" is on larger lines; in design and in character-isation it is a considerable achievement. It holds your interest cunningly, though there is scarcely a likeable person in the book, and one of its triumphs is, that though she is scarcely likeable and brings her worst troubles on herself by her own indis-cretions, the chief character in the book, Amy Steevens, is so natural a human creature and goes her way so courageously that the reader is subtly drawn into sympathising with her. She was "con-stitutionally a rolling stone"; had been assistant in a dressmaker's shop and in a typewriting establish-ment; secretary to a literary man, and companion to a lady, and had been on the stage. She had been to South Africa and, as a famous man's

amanuensis, to Russia. When the novel opens she is
serving as governess or companion to the young
daughter of an English family staying in Paris. Her
native unconventionality is always betraying her into
difficulties. When Sir Mervyn Dymond, a worried
co-respondent in a divorce suit, attempts to commit
suicide, she compromises herself by dashing upstairs
and into his bedroom to save him, and is dismissed
from her situation accordingly. To atone for this,
Sir Mervyn takes her to London as his secretary,
and she compromises herself further by staying in
his house there, though the relations between them
remain on an entirely blameless business footing.
Without beauty or passion, she has personality;
men are strangely attracted to her, and she has to
fight her way very much as Becky Sharp did, and
is not always so successful as Becky in contending
with the human animals who beset her. Not a
pleasant story, but written with imaginative realism
and with marked ability.

This book was published in 1908, the year, as
Miss Hunt notes in "The Flurried Years", which
began for her "with such high hopes, both personal
and literary. . . . As a literary woman, my years
of mark and usefulness coincided with a great
literary launch, that of the 'greatest Review in the
world'", which proud title she gives to the *English
Review*, founded under the editorship of Ford

Madox Hueffer in 1908. She touches in some amusing pictures of the unpretentious manner in which the editorial work was carried on in the offices over a poulterer's and fishmonger's shop in Holland Park Avenue. She had written three short stories which an agent had returned to her because he had been unable to sell them and, on the advice of H. G. Wells, she called at the office of the *English Review* and offered them to the editor, and he accepted the second, "The Coach", without reading it.

Presently she became reader for the *Review*, and as such had the luck to discover D. H. Lawrence. "The editor handed me some manuscript poems," she says, "written in pencil and very close, which had come to him from a young schoolmistress in the Midlands. She said that her sweetheart was schoolmaster in the same school. He was the son of a miner, and not very strong, but she had copied out some of his poems, and would the editor give them a glance."

Editor and reader rejoiced in this discovery of a new genius; the poems went into the *Review*, and after some correspondence Lawrence came up to London, abandoned schoolmastering, and started on his literary career. In those days, in addition to being much occupied with the *Review* and with social engagements, Violet Hunt took an active part in the suffragette movement, and tells how she and May

132

VIOLET HUNT

Sinclair stood outside High Street, Kensington, railway station with collecting boxes, gathering funds for the cause. In all those "Flurried Years", when she was busy in these ways, travelling abroad at intervals, and continually worried with the care of an invalid mother and all manner of domestic and other anxieties, though she says nothing of her books, beyond casually mentioning the names of about two of them, she was finding time to write another seven or eight. "The Doll" (1911) was followed by "The Desirable Alien", which caused the German police to keep a cautious eye on her when she was visiting Germany shortly after its publication in 1913. Then came, in 1915, "The House of Many Mirrors", and "Their Lives", in 1916, with its continuation, "Their Hearts", in 1921, and between these two, "The Last Ditch", in 1918. Another book of short stories, "More Tales of the Uneasy", in 1925, was succeeded a year later by that curiously intimate chronicle of her own tumultuous experiences, "The Flurried Years", which I value most for its interesting personal recollections of so many of her famous contemporaries—of Conrad, Henry James, and more than all, and to say nothing of others, of W. H. Hudson. I don't think Violet Hunt has drawn any character, real or imaginary, with more insight, more beautifully sympathetic understanding than she draws Hudson's

K   133 in the last twenty pages of this book. Into those few pages she gets a wonderfully living picture of him, his appearance, his way of life, his habits of thought, the resentful mood in which he met old age and the approach of death; these things leading to a poignant account of his dying, of her going to his house, when all the blinds along the street were down, and standing in the unfamiliar silence of the familiar room where he lay dead, and to the final scene of the funeral, where the mourners, little incongruities of incident that edged the solemnity of the occasion, are all etched in with the minutely detailed realism of a Pre-Raphaelite painting. One had not expected so gracious an ending to so bitter and stormy a book as "The Flurried Years", and it comes there like the windless quiet that fell when last night's storm had worn itself out

"and in one place lay
Feathers and dust, to-day and yesterday."

ALDOUS HUXLEY

ALDOUS HUXLEY appeared above the horizon and stepped into the world of letters, in 1916, at the early age of twenty-two. He arrived from Eton and Balliol with their distinctive labels still on his baggage and, son of the distinguished author and editor Leonard Huxley, grandson of the great scientist Thomas Henry Huxley and linked on his mother's side to the great poet and critic Matthew Arnold, he came with the prestige of a famous ancestry to clear the way before him. But though in our social world a man's forefathers may give place and honour and precedence even to one who is no more than

"the tenth transmitter of a foolish face,"

in the literary world the most they can do for him is to give him an excellent send-off; if he cannot do the rest for himself he soon drops to his proper level and remains there. Every author is necessarily a self-made man, and, lacking the ability to make himself, he gets no inheritance from his fathers, in the end, but the right to sleep with them.

135

THE GLORY THAT WAS GRUB STREET

Possibly Aldous Huxley inherited some of his qualifications, but he has acquired enough of his own to render him independent of collateral distinctions. Arriving in 1916, on "Burning Wheels", he has advanced rapidly at the head of a brilliant procession of books in verse and prose which is still lengthening behind him. "Burning Wheels" was followed in 1918 by "The Defeat of Youth"; by "Limbo" and "Leda" in 1920; "Crome Yellow" in 1921; "Mortal Coils" and "On the Margin" in 1922; "Antic Hay" in 1923; "Little Mexican" in 1924; "Those Barren Leaves" in 1925; and "Essays Old and New" and that admirable chronicle of a pilgrimage in the East and to America, "Jesting Pilate", in 1926.

Twelve books in ten years—poems, essays, short stories, three novels and one book of travels—all before he was thirty-three; and as the dazzling procession passed it was greeted with acclamations loud enough to drown the outcries, here and there, of any scandalised dissenters. He was praised as a thinker, a scholar, a writer whose verse and prose had grace and charm and a delicate finish of style; who could turn from fantasy and classical myth to the sordid and sometimes gross activities of the human animal in the sophisticated world of to-day and could touch the squalor and meanness of such lives with occasional beauty of thought and phrase,

which, by the way, are no more inherently theirs
than the glory that comes to it when it happens to
reflect the sunlight is the property of the cesspool.
He was hailed as the last word in modernity, a
splendid rebel against convention, an artist, a realist
who boldly painted ugly truths in their native colours
and tore aside those reticences with which, to his
thinking, an hypocrisy or false delicacy, commonly
practised in literature, veils what are convention-
ally known as the lusts of the flesh. And much
of this praise was unquestionably due to him;
he had the art to adorn some of the unloveliest
themes he took in hand, but whether some of
them were worth adorning still remains an open
question.

Always this doubt has been a respectful under-
tone in the general chorus of praise. His critics
have deplored his tendency to lapse at times into a
mere coarseness of language, to indulge now and
then in "genial blasphemies", to give undue prom-
inence in his tales of men and women to their
sexual relationships. You may say it is nothing
against his books if there are things in them that
would have shocked his aunt, Mrs. Humphrey Ward
—that would have shocked most people who were
brought up in the too-narrow Victorian tradition of
social and literary propriety; but the critics who
have deprecated his extravagances have not all been

old-fashioned or elderly—critics of the new generation, themselves at war with conventions, have
suggested, purely on artistic grounds, that he allows
himself too much licence in these matters. After
all, the sexual functions, their use and abuse, are
as much commonplaces of human experience as was
the proverbial philosophy of Martin Tupper, and to
expound the obvious in any kind does not indicate
that a writer has either originality of outlook or a
knowledge of life. Of course there are plenty of
men and women who have no morals, or no more
intelligent self-restraint in the exercise of their pro-
creative aptitudes than have cats or dogs: everybody
knows that, and it is only the inexper.enced who
are too surprised to keep quiet about it; but these
raw children of nature are a minority in civilised
communities, otherwise society would be a chaotic
sort of pig-sty, and the writer who allows them too
much space in his stories is so far from revealing
the whole truth that, by not keeping it within due
proportions and presenting it as a small, unripe part
of a more wholesome whole, he is even distorting
the little truth he shows.

These faults are inevitable faults of youth, to
whom naturally all old things are surprisingly new.
Aldous Huxley began to publish when he was very
young, and over certain of his work is the trail of
the clever undergraduate who is a little too cock-

sure about a world he has not yet had time to explore, and who fully believes he is more sophisticated than he actually is. These immaturities and errors in taste would not be worth mentioning if the mind behind them had not proved itself also rich in other knowledge, endowed with humour and human kindness, finely susceptible to beauty of thought and emotion and subtly skilled in the art of expressing them.

Of his three novels, "Antic Hay" is the best known and the best, I think, in the portrayal of character, in narrative power and in literary quality. There is a far maturer note in it than in "Crome Yellow", which preceded it by two years, though "Antic Hay" is much more flawed by crude preoccupations with sexual traffic. The libidinous adventures of Mr. Mercaptan, Coleman, Rosie, Mrs. Viveash, of the egregious Gumbril, especially the detailed account of Gumbril's ecstatic fumblings over the naked body of the amoral but virginal Emily, smack unpleasantly of that yeasty interval between boyhood and manhood which Keats refers to in his preface to "Endymion".

There is cleverness in the satire and whimsical humour of "Crome Yellow", but it is all a coming and going of people who look like men and women but are not more so than are the figures in a puppet show. They simulate human passions and play at life amusingly as puppets do when their strings are pulled, but they never quicken to any warmth of humanity, so that even the futile Mary's talk of her sex-repressions, her fears that they are dangerous, and her method of dealing with them all seem artificial and harmless. Nothing else in "Crome Yellow" is nearly so good as Mr. Wimbush's history of the dwarf Sir Hercules Lapith and his dwarf wife, Filomena, and their son who grew to the stature of ordinary men and, with his friends, ridiculed and made his parents ashamed of their misfortune. This, which so easily might have been only a quaint, curious fantasy, is curious and quaint but strangely piteous, strangely tragic, and remains in one's memory as a beautifully human interlude in a country house comedy whose actors and their actions are lively but trivial unrealities.

With more of ripeness, there is more of unripeness, or perhaps over-ripeness, in "Antic Hay". But if half-a-dozen of its characters are primitive, unredeemed animals, they are more robustly mortal than any in "Crome Yellow"; and Gumbril's father, that ambitious old architect, and his friend the solid Mr. Porteous are little masterpieces of delightfully humorous characterisation; so is the fashionable tailor with Bolshevik leanings, Mr. Bojanus. The talk between him and Gumbril concerning Gumbril's absurd invention of pneumatic small-clothes is worth all the amorous intrigues and bleary facetious chatter in the book put together. These men and Lypiatt lift it to a higher level; and it is significant that it is Lypiatt, the eccentric, half-mad poet and artist, who gets near the truth about the lives and ideals of most of the persons in "Antic Hay" when Gumbril, Mr. Mercaptan, Coleman and Shearwater are guying him, as they dine together in a Soho restaurant, and he breaks out angrily against their cheap cynicism and airy mockeries:

"You disgust me," said Lypiatt, with rising indignation and making wider gestures. "You disgust me—you and your odious little sham eighteenth-century civilisation; your piddling little poetry; your art for art's sake instead of for God's sake; your nauseating little copulations without love or passion; your hoggish materialism, your bestial indifference to all that's unhappy and your yelping hatred of all that's great."

"Charming, charming," murmured Mr. Mercaptan, who was pouring oil on his salad.

"How can you hope to achieve anything decent or solid, when you don't even believe in decency or solidity? I look about me," and Lypiatt cast his eyes wildly round the crowded room, "and I find myself alone, spiritually alone. I strive on by myself, by myself." He struck his breast, a giant, a solitary giant. "I have set myself to restore painting and poetry to their rightful position among the great moral forces. They have been amusements, they have been mere games too long."

For all his extravagant egoism, Lypiatt holds your sympathy, your liking. He develops into a

141

grotesquely pitiful and tragic figure, is something of a counterpart in fiction to Benjamin Haydon in real life. There is strength of character, a sane manliness and depth of feeling in Lypiatt's wild ravings, which emphasise the lack of those qualities in the flashy witticisms and automatic amours of his friends, those degenerates of the half-world who swagger as men of the world.

Lypiatt makes me wonder whether I am misunderstanding Huxley's purpose and philosophy—whether there is not the scornful satire of a dispassionate but interested looker-on in the unrestrained, sometimes repellant realism of his pictures of the sex-obsessed specimens exhibited in this and other of his stories. Anyhow, I suspect that in Lypiatt's fierce outcry he is letting his private opinions loose and satirising passing tendencies in his own work and tendencies that are passing or permanent in the work of some of his contemporaries.

One ignores the fussy prudery that brands the use of sex problems in imaginative literature as a forbidden sin; but there is more than one way of using them. In "Antic Hay" they are used, apparently, for their own sakes and to no end; they are nothing new; they only disclose what every adult reader knows perfectly well already, and the baldly frank discussion of them leads nowhere. One can admire the candid treatment of such matters when it is done with the object of achieving an artistic effect, as it is in some of Huxley's short stories —in "The Gioconda Smile", for instance. That is a story worth telling, brilliantly told, and depending essentially for its developments on the sexual proclivities of the deftly psychologised Mr. Hutton. One cannot say the same for the sex stories in "Limbo"; but there are finer things elsewhere, notably the title story, in "Little Mexican and Other Stories"; and always Huxley writes with grace and charm and a feeling for the magic of words, even when he is spending his exceptional gifts on themes that are not good enough for them, wasting an exquisite art on subjects that are inherently inartistic.

In his time he has worked for the press as a critic of art, drama and music, and has done a good deal of miscellaneous writing, selections from which have been gathered into his books of essays. These range from a dissertation on pantomime songs to lucid and scholarly studies of Chaucer, Ben Jonson, Sir Christopher Wren. He began as a poet, and has written *vers libre* with a larger sense of its delicate nuances than most English poets seem to possess. He made an early sensation with the stark realism of such poems as "Frascati's", which pictures an evening in that famous restaurant from the point of view of the balcony, the "human bears beneath, champing with their gilded teeth", and the jazz band in full blast, until,

> "when the wearied band
> Swoons to a waltz, I take her hand.
> And there we sit in blissful calm,
> Quietly sweating palm to palm."

There is enough beauty in "Leda" to more than justify Huxley's reputation as a poet; but the best of his poetry, apart from that, is I believe in the little volume of "Selected Poems", published in 1925, from which he has excluded all the startling things that tickled the ears of the very modern groundlings. And I hazard a guess that you get a glimpse of the real Huxley, the man whose spiritual qualities are continually breaking through his materialism, of his self-dissatisfactions, his aspirations, in "The Reef", where he tells how he stands watching the "phantom fish goggling in on me through the misty panes", and feels

> "I am grown less
> Than human, listless, aimless as the green
> Idiot fishes of my aquarium,"

and has a sea-dream of voyaging to great depths and a desired haven where he might find "an endless sequence of joy and speed and power"—a mystic reef where

ALDOUS HUXLEY

                              "the body shall be
Quick as the mind; and will shall find release
From bondage to brute things; and joyously
Soul, will and body, in the strength of triune peace,

Shall live the perfect grace of power unwasted.
And love consummate, marvellously blending.
Passion and reverence in a single spring
Of quickening force, till now never yet tasted

But ever ceaselessly thirsted for, shall crown
The new life with its ageless starry fire.
I go to seek that reef. . . ."

WILLIAM WYMARK JACOBS

IF humour had not been such an insidious quality, a way would long since have been found of vaccinating all humorists when they were young (especially if they were likely to become humorous writers) with something that would have cured them and turned them into serious authors and harmless citizens. But so subtle and apparently inoffensive is it in its operations that few have recognised humour as, like religion, a natural enemy of the power and glory of Important Persons and of whatever perpetuates irreligious distinctions between class and class. Since the foundation of the world, it has been affably undermining the dignities and pomposities of mankind and laughing them out of existence; it has been joyously spreading a gospel of universal brotherhood, exposing the follies of the over-wise, bringing the mighty down from their high mightiness and levelling them with the humble and meek. It is no respecter of persons; the act of laughter is the same in all languages, and wherever men laugh together social differences, at any rate for the time, go all to pieces.

147

THE GLORY THAT WAS GRUB STREET

If the Law had not been the "hass" Mr. Bumble said it was, it would have realised all this ages ago and scheduled humour among the forbidden arts, and in that case, unless he had been caught and converted when young, W. W. Jacobs would, by this, have been martyred in the good cause and we might have had the pleasure of seeing him honoured in one of those stained-glass windows that are at present reserved to public benefactors who serve humanity seriously and with grave faces. Jacobs does it with a grave face all right, and his countenance would have looked perfectly seemly in his window: that is one of the deceptive, disconcerting things in most humorists—they are serious men in themselves, but they upset the seriousness of others.

Jacobs was born in 1863 and began his career with a proper sense of the earnestness of life as we have made it by going as a clerk into the Savings Bank Department of the Post Office. If only he had stayed there and gone on diligently looking after the financial interests of the million he could have risen to such eminence that an O.B.E. or even a knighthood might have been his portion. But the humorist in him broke out and he took to writing short stories in his spare time; I remember the joy I had in reading the very earliest of them in Jerome's magazines *To-day* and *The Idler*, back in the '90's; and he went on doing this and became

a boon and a blessing and a healthful antidote to
the sort of literature that was plentiful in those days
that are supposed to have been given over to the
decadents, and a boon and a blessing he remains
to a generation that has need of all the happiness it
can get. Our various Governments that, of recent
years, have showered honours lavishly on men who
have never done any of us any good, have discreetly
passed him by; but you will notice that such
glittering rewards are never offered to humorists,
perhaps because the powers that be think, like Lord
Froth in Congreve's comedy, that laughter "is such
a vulgar expression of the passion—everybody can
laugh"; or perhaps because they have some instinct
of self-defence and a hazy subconsciousness that
one touch of humour makes the whole world kin,
and too much of it would shatter the last absurdities
of our sorry social scheme and puncture the possi-
bilities of flashy distinction that are still open to
ambitious politicians. Anyhow, as I say, apart
from due wages, Jacobs has received no reward to
date, except the admiration and affection of many
thousands of readers, and, moreover, I am certain
he does not covet any other.

For he is a very modest and retiring man. He
even retired from the Post Office in 1899, when his
third book, "Sea Urchins", had fully established
his popularity. Three years earlier, his first collection

of stories, "Many Cargoes", had been so immediately and emphatically successful that he need not have hesitated, but it was not until a second book, his first novel, "The Skipper's Wooing" (1897) and a third had amply maintained the success of "Many Cargoes" that he felt justified in closing the books of the nation in the Savings Bank Department and setting himself free to write us some more of his own. Another novel, "A Master of Craft", followed "Sea Urchins" in 1900, and since then have come in quick succession "Light Freights", "At Sunwich Port", "The Lady of the Barge", "Odd Craft", "Dialstone Lane", "Captains All", "Short Cruises", "Salthaven", "Sailors' Knots", "Ship's Company", and at longer intervals "Night Watches", "The Castaways", "Deep Waters", and, in 1926, "Sea Whispers".

In all these novels and stories Jacobs has been as faithful to the docks and wharves and waterside districts of London and Essex as Hardy has been to Wessex and, allowing for some farcical extravagances of incident, his quaint old salts and the famous Night Watchman are as true to life as are the peasants of the Wessex novels. A born Londoner, they tell me, and I should have been surprised to hear otherwise, that Jacobs spent much of his younger days in and about the riverside places and little coast towns with whose atmosphere and

picturesque personalities his books have made us
familiar; that he used to voyage aboard such
Thames barges and coasting schooners as glide
through his pages, and was on terms of intimacy,
ashore and at sea, with those captains, mates, able
seamen, cabin boys, watchmen, publicans and other
lively sinners whom he has introduced to us with
such insight and imaginative humour that nowadays
we feel almost as intimate with them as he is. You
cannot easily fit him into that rough and hearty
environment, and you picture him to yourself a
slim, slight, boyish figure, oddly contrasting with
his robust companions, a quiet, grave, reticent
looker-on at the game, an acute observer, a chiel
amongst them making mental notes that, though he
did not know it at the time, he would in due course
print.

He had that boyishness of figure and general
appearance, that thoughtful gravity and shyness of
manner when I first saw him at a public dinner
soon after "At Sunwich Port" had given everybody
something fresh to laugh over; and, except that
his close, smooth hair is changing to an iron-grey,
he has them all yet. Nobody seeing him at one of
the dinners of the pleasant Bohemian club where
he is occasionally to be seen, and not knowing who
he was, would ever guess that he was one of the
greatest of living humorists; they would far more

likely fancy he was a venturesome young curate who, coming unwontedly into unconventional surroundings, that his flock might even consider slightly wicked, had discreetly laid his clerical garb aside and dressed appropriately as one of the ungodly for the occasion. He is a delightfully witty speaker, when he can be persuaded to speak, but that is rarely; I doubt whether any author of his distinction, or of half his distinction, is more seldom heard or seen in public places. He makes his home well away from London, at Berkhamsted, and I have heard from one of his admirers who visited the little Hertfordshire town (where that other quiet man, Cowper, was born), that he collogued with a prominent native who knew no more than the name of Jacobs and was surprised to hear that the tenant of Beechcroft was a famous author. He is as unobtrusive as Tennyson pretended to be; for, having a sense of humour, he does not cultivate eccentricities of behaviour, not even to the extent of going about clothed like a stage brigand.

In addition to a prevailing sense of humour, he has a subtle and potent sense of the weird, the gruesome, the terrible, and a sense of sentiment and pathos, which he employs sparingly and with a touch so light and apparently casual that a careless reader may miss the delicacy of his skill even while he is moved by the effects of it. Mostly his sentiment and humour are so artfully blended that the one is almost indistinguishable from the other. This is very neatly and charmingly done in the closing scene of "The Skipper's Wooing"; and again as neatly and as charmingly in "At Sunwich Port", where young Hardy, having put himself to infinite trouble in the service of the Nugent family in order to ingratiate himself with his irascible enemy, Captain Nugent, and be allowed to visit their house and pay his addresses to Kate Nugent, has at last won the freedom of the premises and is making love to Kate in the garden with a dogged determination that breaks down all her coquettishness:

"If you would do anything to please me," she said at length, in a low voice and without turning her head, "would you promise never to see me or speak to me again, if I asked you?"
"No," said Hardy promptly.

Miss Nugent sat silent again. She knew that a good woman should be sorry for a man in such extremity, and should endeavour to spare his feelings by softening her refusal as much as possible, little as he might deserve such consideration. But man is impatient and jumps to conclusions. Before she was half way through the first sentence he leaned forward and took her hand.

"Oh, good-bye," she said, turning to him with a pleasant smile.

"I'm not going," said Hardy quietly. "I am never going," he added, as he took her other hand.

Several of his novels and stories have these moments of humorous sentiment; "A Master of Craft" has them, and it ends with one of those rare, poignantly pathetic little incidents that Jacobs handles with a deft, elusive art that never fails him, whether he is conjuring for our tears or for our laughter. Captain Flower, a genial man of many loves, has through all his airy infidelities remained faithful to the penniless Poppy Tyrell and is bent on making her his wife. Clearing the way for this, at last, he conspires with his friend, Fred Fraser, to establish a story that he has fallen overboard and been drowned, thinking to disappear and not to return till certain of his charmers, who will not be shaken off, have got engaged to other men. Fraser, acting as his go-between, takes his occasional messages to Poppy, and she and Fraser fall in love with each other, but hide it from each other out of loyalty to him. Presently, he goes to sea; his ship is wrecked, and as his name is not in the list of survivors, Poppy and Fraser assume that he is dead. After a lapse of time he returns and, inquiring at his friend's house, learns that Fraser's marriage is at that moment in progress and is told the name of the bride. He rushes frenziedly to the church, but the wedding is just over before he arrives, and he lingers despair-

ingly with the crowd to see them come out. When
they emerge they see him and are as startled as if
they were looking on one risen from the grave.
Then Poppy gives a sudden cry of joy and amazement
and makes a movement toward him, but to spare
her and cover his misery he snatches some rice from
the bag of an old woman beside him, flings it over
them, backs into the crowd, and hurries away. The
almost grotesque poignancy of the scene is lost in
this summary; you must read it as Jacobs has written
it for that.

Always he writes with restraint, and with a luminous
economy of words, and with a genius for suggesting
twice as much as he tells; nowhere is his own personality obtruded in humorous comments or facetious
asides. His style is austere in its simplicity; the
humour of his stories is not more in their plots
than in their characters, their dialogue, and in the
quietly droll, tersely, and evasively humorous turns
of phrase in which the action is unfolded and the
psychology of his men and women revealed. Many
of the stories dispense with the love interest altogether; when they do not, the heroine is as often as
not a mature widow set upon marrying again, or a
young girl who is hoydenish, very pretty, very
self-possessed and smart at repartee; there is a
family likeness, too, between the pert, irrepressible
boys in Jacobs' diverting collection, but his elder

women and old and young men are amazingly
varied in character, despite the narrow range of
the world to which he restricts himself. The Night
Watchman is the greatest of his humorous creations,
as Falstaff is Shakespeare's. Though the majority
of his tales are compact of unalloyed humour, there
are two or three, notably "The Monkey's Paw"
and "The Brown Man's Servant", which show
him as a master of eerie mystery and horror, who
challenges comparison with Poe; the effect of "The
Brown Man's Servant" is heightened by a wry
humour which Poe had not, and the uncanny
grimness of "The Monkey's Paw" by a pathos
that is wrought to a pitch of almost painful
intensity when the knock comes on the door
at night and the heart-broken mother, after
struggling desperately with the bolts, flings the
door open and there is nothing there. This, like
"Beauty and the Barge" and other of his stories,
has been as successful on the stage as in Jacobs'
books; it is the most perfect thing artistically that
he has done, and so far from agreeing that "he
is only wearisome when he attempts to write in
other veins than the humorous," I have never
ceased to wonder why he has not given us more
stories in this kind, since he is as fine and as effective
an artist in writing them as in writing those joyous
comedies and farces that made him rich at first

156

and keep him so. It is currently preached as a literary dogma that artistic work cannot be popular, and popular work cannot be artistic, but Jacobs has opened a door to heresy, for his books are both.

JEROME K. JEROME

BEFORE starting to write this essay I have been looking into the past trying to remember how we were off for humorists in 1885, and thereabouts. I am not thinking of men who could mix humour, more or less, in a book that would not as a whole be described as humorous, but of men who were writing books that were that, and not meant to be anything else. They had a few in America, like Mark Twain and Max Adler (who is unaccountably neglected nowadays), and here we had W. S. Gilbert, Henry S. Leigh, and others writing in verse, but in prose, apart from F. Anstey, who had burst into roaring popularity with "Vice Versa", in 1882, so far as I can recollect, we were largely dependent on a little group, of which Francis Burnand was one, and they had reduced humour to a formula, turned it into a matter of nothing but fatuous verbal puns that seem too feeble now ever to have had strength enough to tickle people and make them laugh.

That was the state of things in the literary field, with Anstey ploughing a lonely furrow, when Jerome Klapka Jerome began to become an author. He was born at Walsall in 1859 (and shortly before his death Walsall did well in conferring the Freedom of its City upon him, in recognition of his gifts), but his father, who had been a colliery owner, met with financial disaster and migrated with his family to London. Jerome was then four years old, and much of his youth was spent at Poplar, where his father started afresh as a wholesale ironmonger. He had nearly as rough and hard a boyhood and youth as Dickens endured, and those early vicissitudes had their share in moulding both the man and the writer. A knowledge of the seamy side of life is at the heart of his sympathy with the underdog, and often gives point to the jests and genial philosophy of his "Idle Thoughts of an Idle Fellow", as when he says, for example:

"Years ago, when my whole capital would occasionally come down to 'what in town the people call a bob,' I would recklessly spend a penny of it, merely for the sake of having the change, all in coppers, to jingle. You don't feel nearly so hard up with elevenpence in your pockets as you do with a shilling. . . . I can speak with authority on being hard up. I have been a provincial actor. If further evidence be required, which I do not think likely, I can add that I have been a 'gentleman connected with the press.' I have lived on fifteen shillings a week. I have lived a week on ten, owing the other five; and I have lived for a fortnight on a great coat."

If he makes a jest of remembered hardships, that is partly the measure of his courage, and partly because, as he has it in the "Idle Thoughts" essay on Memory, time puts a glamour over the past "and the bitterness and sorrow of to-day are smiled at on the morrow". Anyhow, I am not going to retell the story of those days in detail, for he has told it all perfectly in his autobiographical "My Life and Times", sketching its poignances lightly, realistically, veiling them with touches of wry or whimsical humour, and I feel it should be read in that book and could only be marred by a summary.

For a while, when he was old enough to take a hand in business affairs, he worked, like Pett Ridge, as a railway clerk; his office was at Euston, and Pett Ridge's at London Bridge. He gave that up to follow a natural bent and go on the stage, with no salary for two months; then successively for ten, fifteen and thirty shillings a week. It was an arduous pursuit, but for three years he was acting in London and the provinces, and proved himself a very capable actor too; he played all manner of characters, including every part in "Hamlet", he says, "except Ophelia", and he "doubled the parts of Sairey Gamp and Martin Chuzzlewit on the same evening." He abandoned the footlights to become a "penny-a-liner", but, finding such journalism too precarious, took an appointment as assistant master at a Clapham school for a term, and might have gone from that to be secretary to Herbert Spencer but preferred instead to go as secretary to a builder in North London for a short time. Thereafter, he was clerk to a commission agent, to a firm of Parliamentary agents, and in a solicitor's office. And "all this time," he tells you in "My Life and Times", "I had been writing stories, plays, essays. But it was years before anything came of it."

Yet he was only twenty-six when his first book came of it. He put his experiences as an actor into "On the Stage and Off" and having been rejected by two or three magazines the manuscript was purchased outright for five pounds, for serial purposes, by the *Play*. "It was the first time," writes Jerome, "I had ever possessed a five-pound note." Publishers fought shy of it when it was offered as a book, and at last it was accepted as a gift by the Leadenhall Press and duly made its appearance in 1885. I was one of the prompt buyers of that dumpy book in a pink paper cover and found so much delight in it that I am not surprised to learn it sold fairly well, even though the critics were not particularly kind to it. If it did not yield much in the matter of money, it was a good start, and helped to pave the way for a second book. By this time Jerome had met that friend of so many authors, F. W. Robinson; "The Idle Thoughts of an Idle Fellow" ran serially in his magazine, *Home Chimes*, and in 1889 the book was published by the Leadenhall Press and must have had a quick and large sale, for my copy, bought second-hand well over thirty years ago, bears on the fly-leaf the name of the original purchaser with the date, "October '89," below it, and the cover flaunts the satisfactory words "fortieth edition." The book has its serious moods, but on the whole it was the freshness and drollery and humour of it that captured the public and made it the talk of the town; and when "Three Men in a Boat" came out in that same year Jerome went so phenomenally popular that it was more than the critics could bear; for no self-respecting critic likes to see everybody rushing off to buy a book without waiting for his advice.

I asked Arrowsmith, its publisher, about it some while back, and he said it had sold persistently and well every year since the year of its publication; one of its numerous new editions, in 1909, announces in a publisher's advertisement that it had then reached its two hundred and seventh thousand, so at a modest estimate you may take it that the sales have now mounted to some three hundred thousand and, after a vigorous life of thirty-eight years it is still selling. An Author's note in that 1909 edition mentions that, the book having been published before the Copyright Convention, though it had sold over a million copies in the United States it had brought him no hard cash from that quarter, but he had been compensated by the fame and popularity it had won for him with the American public. It has been translated into very many languages, and has brought him friendly and grateful letters from all sorts and conditions of men and women. "It remains only," writes Jerome in that prefatory note, "to explain the merits justifying such an extraordinary success. I am quite unable to do so. I have written books that have appeared to me more clever, books that have appeared to me more humorous. But it is as the author of 'Three Men in a Boat (to say Nothing of the Dog)' that the public persists in remembering me."

Fortunately nearly everybody knows it, so there is no need to attempt any outline of the joyous, irresponsible story of the voyage up the Thames of the three men and the dog, for it would be difficult to do, since it is a story that is continually digressing into other stories, such as that of how Uncle Podger hung the picture; the adventure with the fashion-plate young lady; the interlude of George's father at the "Pig and Whistle"; the diverting yarn of the plaster-of-Paris trout. . . . It is all a rollicking, riotous farce written by a young man for young men and women and for older folk who have not forgotten that they used to be young and still want to laugh, and still know how to. It established him so firmly as a humorist that it was difficult ever after

JEROME K. JEROME

for him to get the general public to accept him as
anything else. He confirmed the public in this
impression of him with "The Diary of a Pilgrimage"
(1891), and later with a second volume of "Idle
Thoughts", and with "Three Men on the Bummel",
to say nothing of "Told After Supper", and nothing of divers of his plays in the broadly farcical
kind.

Soon after the appearance of "The Diary of a
Pilgrimage" he became an editor and joined Robert
Barr in running that humorous monthly, *The Idler*,
and from 1893 to 1897 edited a humorous weekly
of his own, *To-day*. Of the new authors, humorous
and otherwise, he discovered and introduced in
the pages of *To-day* I have said something elsewhere
in this volume, and shall content myself by adding
we have had no weekly since that has been so
good as that in the variety and literary quality of
its contents. But by now Jerome had been labelled;
he and most of the group he gathered round him
had been dubbed "the new humorists", what they
wrote was indiscriminately called "new humour",
and the terms were not always meant to be compli-
mentary, though why humorists or humour should
be any the worse for being new it is not easy to
understand, except that our critics are a conservative
race, wedded to precedent and averse from change.
Zangwill, one of the group, once commented on

M   165

this "bewildering habit in modern English letters" of "sneering down the humorist—that rarest of all literary phenomena. His appearance, indeed, is hailed with an outburst of gaiety; even the critics have the joy of discovery. But no sooner is he established and doing an apparently profitable business than a reaction sets in, and he becomes a byword for literary crime. When 'Three Men in a Boat' was fresh from the press, I was buttonholed by grave theologians and scholars hysterically insisting on my hearing page after page: later on these same gentlemen joined in the hue and cry and shuddered at the name of Jerome. The interval before the advent of another humorist is filled with lamentations on the decay of humour."

That is simple truth, and commenting on Zangwill's protest, in his autobiography, Jerome mentions that *Punch* was especially indignant with "Three Men in a Boat"—"scenting an insidious attempt to introduce 'new humour' into comic literature. For years 'New Humorist' was shouted after me wherever I wrote. Why in England, of all countries in the world, humour, even in new clothes, should be mistaken for a stranger to be greeted with brickbats, bewildered me." It bewildered others of us who were living in those times, for the term was applied impartially to Jerome and Barry Pain, to Pett Ridge and Zangwill, as if they were all exactly alike and each had not a brand of humour that was distinctively his own.

However this may be, it is certain that those who know Jerome only as a humorist only half know him. I remember going in 1890, I think it was to Terry's theatre, and laughing all through an evening at his joyously irresponsible farce, "New Lamps for Old"; but in 1907 I saw another side of him when I went to the first night of that story of Christ in a London lodging-house, the most poignant and beautiful of his plays, "The Passing of the Third Floor Back". Like every humorist, he takes life seriously; no man lacking a sense of humour can do that; unless he can also see the fun of things he cannot rightly see the sadness of them—he attaches importance to trifles, mistakes pomposity for dignity, finds occasion for gravity in matters that are inherently laughable, imagines that wealth or inherited honour exalts him, condescends to patronise where he should be humble enough to pity and be kind, and is never able to feel the tie of common brotherhood that evens the odds between all who are mortal. You have to be humourless before you can be proud, and any sort of pride walls you in and keeps you ignorant of life outside your own.

You will find Jerome's more serious moods breaking through at intervals in his two "Idle Thoughts"

books; in most of his humorous books; and they
prevail, with a leaven of humour, in such of his
novels as "Anthony John", "All Roads Lead to
Calvary", in that best and most quietly humorous
and charming of them, "Paul Kelver", and in certain
of his short stories, notably in the delicately wrought,
tenderly imaginative "John Ingerfield"; they prevail,
too, in the vigorous, outspoken articles he wrote
on social problems of his day. Next to its abounding humour, the constant note in his work is a broad
sympathy with all sorts and conditions of humanity,
a sensitive understanding of the wrongs and disadvantages under which the less fortunate of us have
to live and labour. And you may learn how he
came by that knowledge and that sympathy if you
read the early recollections he has chronicled in his
"My Life and Times".

STORM JAMESON

SOME years ago, when it was being said that the
writing of fiction was falling more and more into
the hands of women, Miss Margaret Peterson confessed to an interviewer that she hoped this was
not so, because "women are too personal in what
they write, and rely too much on the reproduction
of their own feelings and opinions in their books".
But this is not truer of women novelists than of
men, and whether or not it is to be regretted is
I think open to argument. There may be nothing
of this personal touch in such of Miss Peterson's
novels as "Guilty, My Lord", but I seem to remember it in others. No woman novelist of to-day
writes more objectively or with a stronger imaginative realism in the creation of character and the
designing of a story than does Mrs. Henry Dudeney,
but personal feelings and experiences enter into her
books, on occasion, and so far from detracting anything from them add to their colour and force and
lifelikeness. It was the same in the past with
Dickens, Thackeray and Reade, with Meredith and
Hardy; and in the present with Wells, Barrie,

THE GLORY THAT WAS GRUB STREET

Beresford, Swinnerton, Alec Waugh, Pett Ridge, George Moore—in fact, I should say that entirely impersonal novelists, male or female, are as rare as white blackbirds.

It could not very well be otherwise. The novelist, like the poet, is always consciously or unconsciously writing about himself; he may choose definite models for all his men and women; he may not make them in his own image; yet something of his temperament and personality has gone into his choice of models, and gets into his reproduction of them as inevitably as the personality and temperament of the sculptor expresses itself in his statues, of the painter in his paintings. Some of us insist that fiction should not be propagandist, and have said that novels dealing with problems are essentially bad art. Which seems to suggest that the art is in the material rather than in the handling of it.

There is a certain amount of covert or overt propaganda in some of the novels of Storm Jameson (in "The Clash", for instance, and in "Farewell to Youth"), but it grows out of and is inseparable from the stories; they help you to realise, as you may from the facts in the world round you unless you are too comfortable to be observant of them, the folly and cruelty of war, the chicanery that leads to success and the simple honesty that leads to failure in our social and policital systems. You feel that she never spins a tale that is wholly imaginary; that she is intensely interested in life, and has a passionate sympathy with the majority to whom it means a constant struggle against spiritual and material difficulties, a little happiness, and many disillusions, and that her novels have a breadth of human charity and a prevailing sense of reality because they are so rooted in her personal observations and experiences.

She was born and spent her early years at Whitby, now given over to fishing and holiday visitors, but at one time noted for its ship-building. The industry still lingers there and the fascinating sight of the big ships slowly growing in grace and beauty inspired her first ambition, which was only to be realised much later and then vicariously in "The Lovely Ship", where Mary Hanskye comes into management of her uncle's shipyard. Having completed her education at Leeds University, where she took first-class honours in English literature, Miss Jameson came to London and obtained employment as a writer of advertisements for a firm of publicity agents. In her spare time she was busy on a novel, "The Pot Boils", which appeared about 1919, and I remember it struck me as a first novel of quite uncommon promise, and reviewers in general thought likewise; but Miss Jameson herself has formed a less favourable opinion of it, and I notice that she ruthlessly cut it off from a recent list of her books.

Turning from advertisement writing to journalism, in 1920 she became sub-editor of the *New Commonwealth*, and contributed a number of essays and miscellaneous articles to that paper, the *English Review*, and other periodicals. Somewhere about this date she was studying at the London University and, with a thesis on "Modern Drama in Europe", obtained her degree of M.A.; and I suspect there are memories of those London University days in her second novel, "The Happy Highways", which was published in 1920. There are more men than women in this story, and those who think a woman cannot draw a man should read it before they say that again. There is only one woman in it that matters, and Margaret Douglass, who largely dominates it all, is portrayed, from her girlhood onward, with an insight and subtlety of understanding that leave her most intimately realised: a very woman, complex and baffling, for all her simplicities; entirely feminine and lovable, for all her unconventionalities of outlook, or perhaps because of them. The story is related by Joy Hearne, of himself, his brothers, his many and diverse friends and acquaintance; of his and his brothers' plunge into the unrest and yeasty revolutionary life of London, where they live in Bohemian circles while they are attending as students at King's College, in the Strand. More than all, it is the story of Margaret, whom they had known in their North country days and who, pursuing her own studies at the College, shares rooms with them, until she marries, and then, like other of Miss Jameson's heroines, marries the wrong man. The whole thing is graphically, frankly true to certain phases of modern life. There is much discussion of many things that were agitating the mind of the period—good discussion, full of suggestion, growing naturally out of the course and atmosphere of the story and helping to interpret the psychologies of its men and women. "The Pot Boils" was an interesting start, and with "The Happy Highways" Miss Jameson may be said to have arrived.

"Modern Drama in Europe", with its brilliantly critical, sometimes shrewdly devastating survey of the latter-day drama and dramatists of France, Italy, Russia, Scandinavia, Spain, Germany and England, made it abundantly clear that dramatic criticism had got a new master; such comprehensive knowledge of a difficult subject, and such well-balanced critical faculty were the more extraordinary when you considered that this young Daniel had come to judgment when she was still only about half way through her twenties. But she was not giving up to this

173

art what was meant for another, and her fourth book was a third novel, "The Clash" (1922). This is a rather loosely constructed, episodic, war-time story, shrewd and vigorous in its comment on current affairs and taking for its theme what was almost a commonplace problem of war-time psychology—the liaison between a married woman and a soldier while her husband is on service at the front.

Miss Jameson returns to this theme, with variations and handles it with deeper significance and surer constructive skill in "The Three Kingdoms" (1926), where she uses very effectively some of the experience she gained, while she was writing advertisements, of the business side of London life; and she returns to it again, and again successfully and with wide variations, in her latest novel "Farewell to Youth" (1928). But before "The Three Kingdoms" came another of her novels—"The Pitiful Wife" (1923), which perhaps comes before it not only in chronological order.

There is a wild moorland atmosphere and a queer, sometimes grotesque grimness and violence of character and incident in "The Pitiful Wife" which, for the sake of finding a parallel, one compares with scenes and people of certain of the Brontë novels, and it suffers nothing by the comparison. Storm Jameson has worked independently in the same medium; and there is no more similarity than there is between Hardy and Eden Phillpotts, who each from his own angle and through his own temperament interpret similar phases of rural life and character. There must be some potent effluence from the soil and air of the rugged, stern North country that breeds such men as Storm Jameson's John Trude, who was born in 1842, before "the railway was brought down the valley to the coast", and began to bring "softer manners with it":

> "At fifteen John Trude was able to throw men, tried wrestlers and ten years his elder in sinew and skill. He stood six feet four and his shoulders had a bullock's weight behind their drive. At twenty he could throw a yearling bullock by the horns. Withal he was light on his feet as a cat, and his huge body moved with ease and a swiftness that aided him more than his great strength. He was a master drinker and poured down his huge throat a prodigious deal of liquor without any visible change in speech or manner. . . . He was even-tempered enough, and in anger very cold. A friend that taunted him in a drunken humour had reason to remember both these things."

Trude cowed this friend for a moment with a look, but, deceived by his silence, the drunken babbler presently went on "girning" at him, until suddenly Trude got on his feet:

> "It seemed one movement that lifted him out of the chair, drew back his shoulder blades as a tiger's draw back under the supple skin, and set his great haunches for the spring. The wretch was himself a fine fighter, but he

175

dropped to the blow, with the side of his head broken in from jaw to temple. Trude left him where he fell, to be succoured by a servant who, coming in the morning to open the shutters, found him bloody and raving."

There was an ancient feud between Blackacres and Nethermoor, in the North Riding, and when Trude was twenty-three the Blackacres folk sent Nethermoor a contemptuous invitation to a dance, not supposing they would accept it, but on the night of the dance Trude led a party of men to Nethermoor who broke into the barn, scared the girls from their partners and, greatly outnumbered, overwhelmed their Blackacres rivals in Homeric combat. Incidentally, "Trude took a man by the ankles, and swinging him round and round, cleared a space about himself, then let the wretch slip, so that he hurtled across the room and fell down by the wall. Four men rushed together upon the laughing giant," and he felled two with his left hand, took a third by the throat and flung him down with a twisted neck, and cracked the ribs of the fourth between his two mighty hands and dropped him with the breath squeezed out of his body.

The author of "Guy Livingstone", Ouida, and their descendants have presented us with big, lusty, half-barbaric men who have been physical miracles in this way, but they degenerate in their pages to

mere splendidly improbable figures of melodrama.
John Trude is so cunningly built up, so natural a
product of his ancestry, age and environment, that
in his doughty youth, and in the squalid, grim,
grotesque, bedridden besotted and forbidding old
age into which he gradually sinks after the death
of his wife, Ann, he impresses himself on your
imagination as an abnormal yet curiously real
human creature.

But the "pitiful wife" of the story is Trude's
daughter Jael, who has the elvish beauty and simple
windflower charm of her mother. She and her
brother Judas are left to run wild; Trude neglects
them as completely as he neglects his broad acres
and lets them go to waste; and for their education
and decent clothing the children are indebted to
the kind-hearted intervention of a generous, well-
to-do neighbour. Romance comes to Jael when she
meets Richmond Drew, a young sculptor working
in his father's studio, and before she is twenty they
marry and settle in a wing of Trudesthorp Hall,
the rambling old house that has been the home of
the Trudes for over a century—Trude shut off in
his one untidy room taking no interest in their
arrangements. The passion between these two is
a very human passion, and even to the end retains
such beauty as shone around Milton's archangel a
little damaged. Richmond goes to the war, and

this time it is no matter of an erring wife, for Jael has never a thought of love for any man but her husband. It is Richmond who drifts into an affair with a girl who has up-to-date ideas about the relations between the sexes. When he is home, after the war, he makes an excuse to go away and renew this acquaintance, and thereafter the girl will not let him break away when he is tired of her. Jael is lonely with her children during his absences; she is painfully supersensitive to a subtle change in him, dimly conscious of something wrong. When she discovers a letter from the girl she tells him of her discovery and for a while it seems as if "her wild bright spirit might beat itself to death" against this bitter disillusion. When he strives to convince her that, in spite of his folly, he loves her, had always loved her, had always liked best to be with her, she is reduced to a poignant cry of, "Oh, it isn't true. It can't be true. But I'm grown so poor I must pretend it is". The long drama of suspense and resentment and desire for reconciliation through which these two pass to peace and a renewal of the happiness they had lost is unfolded with a rare delicacy of insight and emotional power.

"The Lovely Ship" and, for certain of its characters—notably the too-honest James Grimshaw, his charming, womanly wife Emily, the pushful, astute politician his brother Daniel and Daniel's odd, sensible, generous Fanny—and for its vivid pictures of social life in London during the war, "Farewell to Youth", deserve as much attention as I have tried to give to "The Pitiful Wife" if space remained. As it is, I can only leave the fact that these six novels have given Miss Jameson so high and sure a place among living novelists to carry its own significance.

STEPHEN LEACOCK

STEPHEN LEACOCK

THE old idea that humorists are very serious persons and mostly melancholy, is only half true. Some of them are quiet, cheerful men, enjoy their own jokes and make themselves pleasant and entertaining even in their domestic circles. But there are all sorts of them, just as there are of people who are not humorous. Some are grave, shy, wistful, dyspeptic, learned or ignorant, irritable, humble, conceited, morose or actively bad-tempered. For all his geniality among his intimates, W. S. Gilbert could be as harsh, surly, cantankerous, on little provocation or none, as if he had no sense of the ridiculous; and charmingly whimsical, as he could be with children, Lewis Carroll was reserved, rather unsociable, and, if not ashamed of his delightful stories for children, far more proud of his scholastic achievements. There is an anecdote that when Queen Victoria received him and said how she had loved "Alice in Wonderland" and asked him to send her a complete set of his writings, he went away and presented her only with a set of those mathematical works to which he had put his own name of Charles Lutwidge Dodgson.

THE GLORY THAT WAS GRUB STREET

The unthinking seem surprised when they learn that Stephen Leacock is a Professor of Political Economy, and that the Universities have made him three different sorts of Doctor; but there is nothing surprising about it at all. Extremes meet; both Lamb and Dickens confessed that some incongruous emotion almost impelled them to laugh at funerals, and I am told that when off duty undertakers are the jolliest of men; so it is likely that too much of what Disraeli called "the dismal science" of political economy drives the scientist to find relief in developing a sense of humour. And if Stephen Leacock was asked by the King to let him have a set of his books I am satisfied that he would not respond with a gift of such works as his "Elements of Political Science"; for he does not hide under a pseudonym when he wants to be funny, but takes a healthy and proper pride in the books that have made him famous. He admits, in a preface to "The Garden of Folly", that "if a man has a genuine sense of humour he is apt to take a somewhat melancholy, or at least a disillusioned view of life. Humour and disillusionment are twin sisters." Which is only to say that humour, like X-rays, breaks through the show of things, through social importances, transitory dignities, all kinds of glory, and realises how little is in them and how laughable they are, strutting in the face of death and eternity. This

182

acutely realistic vision gives the humorist his strain
of seriousness; but humour is an attribute of sanity,
and saves him from the folly of taking even his own
seriousness too seriously. Also in that same preface
Leacock says,

"I cannot but think that the true manner of the comedian
is that of smiles and laughter. If I am to be amused let
me see on the stage before me, not the lantern jaws of
sorrow, but a genial countenance shaped like a map of the
world, lit with spectacles, and illuminated with a smile.
Let me hear the comedian's own laughter come first and
mine shall follow readily enough, laughing not at him, but
with him."

That is Leacock's own way of humour. I heard
him talking in public two or three times when he
was visiting this country and can testify that he
laughs while he jokes, as if he were thoroughly
enjoying the jest and, his wit and drollery being the
genuine articles, his audiences laughed louder than
he did; but his laugh is so infectious they would
have had to laugh, anyhow, so he had them both
ways. But though he does not follow the distinctive
American platform fashion, set by Artemus Ward
and Mark Twain, of saying his funniest things without a smile, he is in general, distinctively American
in the humour of his books. There are fundamental
differences between the English and the American
sense of humour. "The Englishman loves what

is literal," writes Leacock, in one of his "Essays and Literary Studies". "His conception of a 'funny picture' is the drawing of a trivial accident in a hunting field, depicting exactly everything as it happened, with the discomfited horseman dripping with water from having fallen into a stream; or covered with mud by being thrown into a bog. The American funny picture tries to convey the same idea by exaggeration. Pushed too far," he says, "British literalism becomes insipid, and American exaggeration runs to seed and is too extravagant to be amusing. A large part of American humour lacks profundity, and wants that stimulating aid of the art of expression which can be found only among a literary people. . . . The British people, essentially a people of exceptions, produce a high form of humorous literature because of their literary spirit, and in spite of the fact that their general standard of humorous perception is lower. In the one case humour forces literature. In the other literature forces humour."

There is truth in this, especially if you take a little from each statement and mix it in with the other; for there has been burlesque and extravagance in English art and literature from the days of the old miracle plays, down through Gilray, Rowlandson, Cruikshank and some of the books they illustrated to our own time; and American humour has always

STEPHEN LEACOCK

had its reasonable leaven of "literalism". This
leaven is in Leacock's humour—in his essays, in that
delightfully whimsical book, "Sunshine Sketches
of a Little Town", scattered through most of his
books, though in most of them, such as "Nonsense
Novels", "Literary Lapses", "The Garden of
Folly", "Moonbeams from the larger Lunacy",
"The Hohenzollerns in America", he lets himself
loose in the vein of extravagant, irresponsible farce
that we have come to call typically American.

Yet he is by birth an Englishman, and one may
assume that his share of the "literary spirit" which
he says is the peculiar inheritance of the English
accounts for his occasional literalism, his shrewd
irony, his moods of seriousness and, perhaps, his
passion for political economy. He was born at
Swanmoor, in Hampshire, in 1869, and was taken
to Canada by his parents when he was seven years
old. His father settled down as a farmer in Ontario,
but the farm paid so badly that Stephen Leacock
and his brothers were "driven off the land and have
become professors, business men and engineers"
He was educated at Upper Canada College, Toronto,
and, having graduated at the University of Toronto
in 1891 went back to the College and for eight years
worked there as a teacher, and finding it "the most
thankless and the worst paid profession in the world,"
gave it up in disgust, and went to the University

185

to study economics and political science, secured a Fellowship, and took his degree of Doctor of Philosophy in 1903. These facts I am distilling from the autobiography with which Stephen Leacock prefaces his "Sunshine Sketches of a Little Town", but there he handles the subject with something of satire and frivolity, and I have tamed it into sober English.

He goes on to record that, after he became a D.Ph.—"from this time, and since my marriage, which had occurred at this period, I have belonged to the staff of McGill University, first as lecturer in Political Science, and later as head of the department of Economics and Political Science". He describes that as one of the prizes of the profession, and adds, "the emolument is so high as to place me distinctly above the policemen, postmen, street-car conductors, and other salaried officials of the neighbourhood, while I am able to mix with the poorer of the business men of the city on terms of something like equality".

But this is not to be taken as an indication that he is soured and embittered and doesn't think life worth living, for all that's left behind him long ago. He is still at McGill's, wrestling with political economy, but, starting in 1910 with "Literary Lapses", he has by now published a score of books that have tickled Great Britain, Canada, America, and other places where they laugh, and made him one of the most popular of modern humorists. And that he is perfectly happy about it and not fretted by any disappointment that the author in him has eclipsed the professor you may gather from his joyous proclamation, in his autobiography, that "personally, I would sooner have written 'Alice in Wonderland' than the whole Encyclopædia Britannica".

I met a man of letters the other day who assured me he could not read Stephen Leacock; he had tried more than once, and could not do it. That was to be expected. There is more than one road to happiness. I have seen strong men moved to tears by the singing of the Frothblowers' Anthem, and there is no sort of humour that is recognised as such by everybody. There are times when, like Homer, Leacock nods; when his extravagances seem forced and mechanical; when he offers you all the ingredients of humour but has not mixed them with any spirit, and you begin to think he has been over-rated. Herrick said he was not every day in the mood to write poetry; and, being popular as he is, and contracts being what they are, you may depend that Stephen Leacock sits down some days to be funny when he is not in the mood for it. There are forced, flat bits in "The Hohenzollerns in America" and in "Frenzied Fiction", but there

187

is enough of genuine, lively, witty farce in both
to make atonement for this. I think, too, some
readers are baulked by the fact that when Leacock
talks he laughs and the world laughs with him
easily, but when he writes he often adopts the
deceptively serious tone that is characteristic of
American humorists when they talk. Take, for
example, that story of "A Little Dinner with
Mr. Lucullus Fyshe", in "Arcadian Adventures of
the Idle Rich". He opens as staidly as if he were
going to write a novel of ordinary social life: "The
Mausoleum Club stands on the quietest corner of
the best residential street in the city". He makes
use, throughout, of a good deal of that "literal"
humour he ascribes to the English, but he punctuates
it with lively satire, and fantastic extravagances of
statement or description are continually breaking
through.

The Duke of Dulham, financially embarrassed,
has gone to America in the hope of being able to
borrow money, and Mr. Fyshe has arranged to
entertain him at the Mausoleum Club under the
impression that he has money to invest:

"The Duke was really a poor man—not poor in the
American sense, where poverty comes as a sudden blighting
astringency, taking the form of an inability to get hold of
a quarter of a million dollars, no matter how badly one needs
it, and where it passes like a storm-cloud and is gone; but

poor in that permanent and distressing sense known only to the British aristocracy. . . . The Duke was so poor that the Duchess was compelled to spend three or four months every year at a fashionable hotel on the Riviera simply to save money, and his eldest son, the young Marquis of Beldoodle, had to put in most of his time shooting big game in Uganda, with only twenty or twenty-five beaters and with so few carriers and couriers and such a dearth of elephant men and hyena boys that the thing was a perfect scandal. The Duke indeed was so poor that a younger son, simply to add his efforts to those of the rest, was compelled to pass his days in mountain climbing in the Himalayas, and the Duke's daughter was obliged to pay long visits to minor German princesses, putting up with all sorts of hardship."

His seat "was practically shut up, with no one in it but servants and housekeepers and tourists . . . and the town house, except for the presence of servants and tradesmen and secretaries, was absolutely shut. But the Duke knew that rigid parsimony of this sort, if kept up for a generation or two, will work wonders, and this sustained him." In New York he meets Viscount Belstairs, who advises him, from experience, that the best way to borrow money in America is to ask for a hundred thousand straight out across the dinner table, "just as you'd ask for a match," and the Duke goes to the Mausoleum Club resolved to do this.

At the Club he is welcomed by Mr. Fyshe and by Mr. Furlong, the rector of St. Asaph's, who is to dine with them, "and after a few minutes he

called the rector 'Furlong,' for he had been familiar
with the Anglican clergy in so many parts of the
world that he knew that to attribute any peculiar
godliness to them, socially, was the worst possible
taste". But a lightning strike of the Club staff,
in common with all the waiters and cooks throughout
the city prevents the dinner, and deprives the Duke
of an opportunity which never returns. How Mr.
Fyshe realises what the Duke is after and deftly
switches him on to another financier, who astutely
avoids negotiations and carries him off, with rifles
and game-bags, to shoot timber wolves in the
Wisconsin woods, and the Duke happily, excitedly,
forgets business at the prospect of pleasure, is told
in the deftest, wittiest farcical comedy manner, and
is the more joyously funny because under all its
burlesque it is a drastic criticism of life as some of
us really live it. Leacock translates his philosophy
into laughter, but it is philosophy none the less.
His irrepressible feeling for the ridiculous keeps him
from treating absurdities as if they were not absurd;
but when he is writing nonsense he knows he is
and puts more wisdom into it than you will find
in the pretentious psychological stories and unsmiling essays of many who, trying to write sense,
write nonsense without knowing it.

E. V. LUCAS

FOR the last half-hour I have been sitting with a
sheet of paper in front of me urging myself to start
writing about E. V. Lucas, but quite unable to make
up my mind where I ought to begin or when and
where I ought to leave off. For he has written
fifty or sixty books—of travel, of stories, of art
criticism, of essays, of biography, one play and
half a dozen books for children; and this says
nothing of six anthologies he has compiled, nor of
books he has edited. Also there is his very first
book, a book of verses all about cricket, called
"Songs of the Bat", which I fancy he must have
called in and suppressed, for it no longer appears
in lists of his works. How many of his miscellaneous contributions to *Punch*, and of those charming little essays he has for some years past been
writing every week for the *Sunday Times*, still
remain uncollected I do not know. On top of all
these and other activities, he was for many years
reader and adviser to the publishing house of
Methuen & Co., and is now Chairman of its board
of directors.

THE GLORY THAT WAS GRUB STREET

I have met him only twice: once when we were both of a small party that dined at the house of Thomas Seccombe, long since; and more recently when the Elian club was founded and its indefatigable secretary, F. A. Downing, induced him to attend one of its dinners at Middle Temple Hall, but has never succeeded in luring him to another. Lucas loves neither public speaking nor literary society. Not that he is anything of a recluse, but that he prefers to go out and about into all sorts of unliterary society where he can find material to his hand which he could not have found by staying at home or by passing his time in clubs and places where only his fellow craftsmen congregate. He knows London as thoroughly as if he had been a born Cockney, and has put the results of his explorings and researches into "A Wanderer in London", and other books. He has gone farther afield for the gossipy history and topography of "Highways and Byways of Sussex", and farther still for the sketches, impressions and miscellaneous lore in those admirable chronicles of "A Wanderer" in Paris, in Venice, in Florence, in Holland, in Rome, in "Roving East and Roving West" and "A Wanderer Among Pictures". His roving West took him to America about eight years ago, not on a lecture tour but to see the country and the people, and Robert Cortes Holliday, who met him in

E. V. LUCAS

Chicago, gives this capital pen portrait of him in his "Men and Books and Cities". Holliday describes him as looking—

> "A youngish fifty, perhaps. Rather tall. A good weight, not over heavy. Light on his feet, like a man who has taken his share in active field games. Something of a stoop. A smile, good, natural, but sly. Dark hair, shot with grey. Noble prow of a nose. Most striking note of all, that ruddy complexion, ruddy to a degree which (as I reflect upon the matter) seems to be peculiar to a certain type of Englishman."

Holliday's guess at his age was, at that date, not far out, for Lucas was born in 1868; he was just twenty when he sent some satirical verses to the *Globe* and made his first appearance in print. A little later, while he was a student at University College, London, he began contributing "By the Way" paragraphs to the same paper, and, like so many young authors of that day, served his apprenticeship as an essayist by contributing to it also his tale of *Globe* turnovers, so called because they filled the last column on the front page and continued for half a column overleaf. A modest fee of a guinea was paid for each of those essays, and the literary free lance lost one of his readiest markets when the *Globe* discontinued that feature shortly before its death. Presently he took a regular engagement on the *Globe's* staff, and remained there

I believe for several years, but already he was making progress in other directions, and journalism was not to be his goal.

In his leisure from journalistic work he had written a book about certain of Charles Lamb's circle, "Bernard Barton and His Friends", to be followed, after an interval of a few years, by "Charles Lamb and the Lloyds"; these preluding his complete edition of Lamb's works and that "Life of Charles Lamb" which have ranked Lucas with the ablest and most brilliant of contemporary editors and biographers. He has left nothing for future editors of Lamb to do. Never, surely, was an author more interestingly or exhaustively annotated and interpreted than Elia is in Lucas's illuminating notes to the essays, letters, poems and plays and miscellaneous writings; they add appreciably to your knowledge of Lamb, his friends and his times, to a more intimate understanding of much that he has written, and are, in short, neither less nor more than such notes ought to be but too seldom are.

But we have gone ahead too quickly, if we are to have any respect for chronology. Somewhere about 1897 Lucas had adventured, with the success that seems to wait upon all his doings, into a very different field and published "A Book of Verses for Children", which was in due season succeeded by "Another Book of Verses for Children", and by other delightful books written for the little people, such as "Anne's Terrible Good Nature", "The Slowcoach" and "The Flamp". And in between these, in 1899 came the first of his anthologies, "The Open Road", and this and "The Friendly Town", "Good Company", and four more have won such laurels for him in this line that most other anthologists now toil after him in vain, and the praise the critics give them is generally diluted with a hint that unfortunately they have not got the Lucas touch— a kind of admonition to "go to the Lucas, thou dullard, consider his ways and be wiser". And the Lucas touch is something too elusive to be defined. You feel it in these anthologies, as you do in his essays, but you cannot pin it down and give it a definition. It may be he is so sensitive to the joy of life—and, by the way, "The Joy of Life" is the title of the latest of his anthologies (1927)—that, in making his choice, he is drawn to the beautifully joyous as well as to the serenely beautiful things in literature, and has read so widely, with a taste so finely catholic that he instinctively gathers every variety of loveliness into his collection, mignonette and the daisy no less than roses and orchids, and has the art of ranging them in a pattern where the homeliest are as perfectly in keeping as are the most exotic. No man who is only a scholar should try to compose an anthology.

195

THE GLORY THAT WAS GRUB STREET

Anthologies are not meant for scholars but for the general reader who is human enough to find pleasure in every degree of worthy prose and verse that, in old Samuel Daniel's phrase, can "give delight and move and sway the affections of men", and unless a man's scholarship is mitigated with as large an interest in life as in literature, with an easy knowledge of his fellows, their tastes and their needs, as well as of books, he is wasting his time in compiling an anthology—to do it properly is beyond his capacity. Those old Elizabethan anthologies, the first in the language, are recognised by the best judges as the true models; half the things in them have long been dead and were never great, but even in their embalmed condition they are fragrant with the spirit of their time and, you may depend, would not have been saved among greater, less mortal verse if they had not chimed with contemporary taste and made some sure appeal to contemporary thought and emotion. It is not the anthologist's business to assume that there can be no good taste except his own; it is his business to realise that he is working for readers of diverse tastes and temperaments, and if his conception of what is good is hopelessly narrowed to what is good for himself he has mistaken his vocation. As an anthologist, E. V. Lucas emphatically knows his business, being gifted with the breadth of sympathy essential to that knowledge, and in the result his anthologies are not only among the best of their kind, but they are popular—as any anthology, to fulfil its object, must be.

While "The Open Road" was in the first bloom of its popularity he won another reputation with that whimsical, farcical, blithely satirical skit on a number of topical things and people (written in collaboration with C. L. Graves) "Wisdom While You Wait". This had all the town laughing, and set a fashion which other humorists followed, but none of them quite recaptured the fine careless rapture of merriment that gave "Wisdom While You Wait" such a vogue that you could scarcely go anywhere without seeing people reading it or without meeting somebody who was thirsting to tell you some of its jokes.

Then, though it came, I fancy, much later (for I am lost among the dates of all these books) there is that book beloved by cricketers, "The Hambledon Men"; there is a biography of E. A. Abbey; studies of Constable and Vermeer of Delft, and the series of excellent little books on great painters. And before and after and in between all these came the thirty or so volumes of novels and essays that, with his work on Lamb, will, perhaps, in the long run remain as his most characteristic and enduring achievement.

THE GLORY THAT WAS GRUB STREET

I cannot be certain whether "Listener's Lure" was the first of his stories, or novels, or "entertainments" as I seem to remember he once labelled them himself, but it was certainly one of the earliest. It arrived so long ago as 1906 and introduced a fresh and refreshing note into the fiction of its period. It adopted the old, well-worn method of telling a story in a collection of letters; but no method is too old in the hands of one who knows how to make it new again, and Lucas had the secret of doing that. Here, as in all his novels, the essayist and the novelist work in collaboration; the characters—Lynn Haberton, the literary man, his ward, Edith Graham, who is also his secretary, the delicate Albourne, the talkative, agnostic, Mrs. Pink, and the rest of the men and women, married and single, of their acquaintance—reveal themselves, or are revealed, and carry on the story in their correspondence; a story with no lack of love interests, abounding in humour, but with moods of deep seriousness, the letters digressing now and then into literary criticism, into gravely or whimsically shrewd comments on life and death and social and moral questions with which everybody is more or less concerned. These cunningly blended elements, and the skill and subtly humorous truthfulness with which the characters are drawn disguise the slightness of the story itself so that it keeps you as closely interested as if it were unravelling a powerful plot, and moves you to repeated chucklings of quiet enjoyment.

This same blend of delightful humour and occasional seriousness of thought, the same blend of essay and story, in varying proportions, the same deftness and lightness of touch and realistic art in characterisation are the irresistible lure of the witty and charming "Over Bembertons", of "Advisory Ben", "Genevra's Money", "Verena in the Midst", "The Vermilion Box" (another tale told in letters, the vermilion box being the familiar pillar-box), "Mr. Ingleside", "Landmarks" (which has a good deal of autobiography in it), and of the Lucas novel in general. Some have more fantasy, or more sentiment, a more everyday homeliness or a more settled plot than others, but the same gracious Lucasian whimsicality and philosophy, acute and sympathetic understanding of men and women and charm of style link them each to each, and would seal them as distinctively his even if no name were printed on their title pages.

As for the essays, their very number and infinite variety reduces me to despair of saying anything of them in the space that remains to me that shall be sufficiently comprehensive. They have all the airy magic of the novels, sometimes are a compromise between tale and essay, and whether they take a theme that drifts into thought that is deep enough for tears, or is lively with burlesque laughter, or lighter in idea than thistledown or almost as intangible as the air, they are as delicately done as any filagree carving in ivory, but have a genial, friendly, companionable warmth of humanity in them that makes the comparison with ivory inadequate. His admirers used to be amazed that Swift could sit down and write an essay on a broomstick; but Lucas does not require a broomstick, he can write a delightfully quaint, witty or wise essay on nothing at all. He has not been contented to travel the great highways of literature, but has an extensive and peculiar acquaintance with its byways, and a special weakness for oddities of literary character, and can fascinate a reader with his cunning re-creations of them. I remember his "Boswell of Baghdad", and, for example, his "Philosopher that Failed" (in "Character and Comedy")—which takes that old Barnard's Inn solicitor, Oliver Edwards, who had been at Pembroke College with Dr. Johnson and is a transitory figure in Boswell's Life, and reconstructs his character, his one meeting with Johnson when they were both old, and by sly little deductions and reasonable amplifications makes the man and the scene more vivid and intimately alive than Boswell himself has made it.

See how the manner and tone, the geniality, and

variableness of the essays get into their very titles—
"Urbanities", "Fireside and Sunshine", "One Day
and Another", "Loiterers' Harvest", "Giving and
Receiving", "Luck of the Year", "Encounters
and Diversions", "Events and Embroideries"—you
know what to expect as soon as you read the names
on the covers, and they do not disappoint you.
Probably because of his association with Elia, Lucas
is occasionally spoken of as if he had chosen Lamb
for his model, but he is no more an imitator of
Lamb than Lamb was of Addison and Steele; he
is his own man, his humour, fantasy, pathos, and
general outlook on men and things are his own,
his subjects his own and his manner of treating
them, and if he has affinities with Lamb, Leigh
Hunt, Addison and Steele, it is simply because, as
an essayist, he is in the legitimate line of descent
from them. But to put this opinion on broader,
more responsible shoulders than mine, I will leave
the last word with the late Sir Edmund Gosse,
who has said in one of his essays: "Unless my
judgment is much at fault, there has written in
English, since the death of R. L. Stevenson, no
one so proficient in the pure art of the essayist as
Mr. E. V. Lucas. . . . There have not been many
true essayists, even in English, but Mr. Lucas is
one of them."

ROBERT LYND

EVERY now and then somebody expresses a cheerful opinion that there is a revival of interest in the essay; but, so far as one can see, the essay has never fallen out of favour since Addison and Steele made it popular by broadening its scope and deftly shortening it to a familiar, entertaining ten-minutes' gossip. Some of Bacon's essays are short enough, but they do not seek to be merry as well as wise; Cowley's have a cultured, leisured charm that makes no particular appeal to the man in the street, but Steele and Addison brought the essay home to every man by simplifying it into a brief and easily readable article about his own affairs—dealing with current problems, with fashions of the moment, sketching a character, telling a story, criticising a book, describing London scenes and events, chronicling excursions into the country, moralising on vices or follies, philosophising on life at large —handling the gravest or most trivial themes, so long as they were of common interest, and doing it all, seriously or humorously, with a grace of style and simplicity of diction that pleased all sorts of

readers because, as all good literature should, it
satisfied the requirements of persons of taste without
being above the heads of average men.

Addison's *Tatler* and *Spectator*, with nothing in
each issue but one of those ten-minute essays, were
to the breakfast tables of the eighteenth century
very much what the newspapers have been on the
breakfast tables and in the railway trains of the
centuries that followed. With the *Rambler*, *Idler*,
Bee, *Looker-On*, *Lounger*, *Tea Table*, *Connoisseur*,
Adventurer, *Guardian*, and other such papers, scores
of periodical essayists followed, more or less successfully, in the *Spectator's* footsteps, and when newspapers developed and captured the public with their
ampler, miscellaneous fare, though the essay as a
separate daily or weekly came to an end, it was
adopted in one form or another as an attractive
addition to the best of them.

The art of writing these short essays is not so
easy as it may seem, and when they are gathered
into a volume it is no longer customary, as it was
down to a few years ago, to dismiss them slightingly
as "reprinted articles", as if it might be taken for
granted they were as ephemeral as the newspapers
in which they first appeared. So much good
literature of this kind has arrived in books by way
of the daily or weekly press that nobody except
the very superior, who are of no consequence, think

any the worse of it now for doing so. Particularly as the periodical essayists of our day include some of the most brilliant of contemporary authors, most of whom are also poets, or novelists, or biographers, or all three.

Wells and Arnold Bennett, Frank Swinnerton, J. B. Priestley, A. A. Milne, Gerald Gould and Hilaire Belloc have all, at intervals, done notable work as periodical essayists; but none more fully and ably maintains the Addison tradition than do G. K. Chesterton, E. V. Lucas and A. G. Gardiner ("Alpha of the Plough"), unless it is Robert Lynd, who began writing these periodical essays twenty years ago and latterly has published one or two a week for well over a decade and has already filled seventeen books with them, and is still under fifty.

He was born at Belfast, the son of a Presbyterian minister, Dr. R. J. Lynd, and you may get some delightful glimpses of his childhood from his first book "Irish and English: Portraits and Impressions" (1908)—a book of essays he had contributed to divers weekly journals, most of them written, as he remarks in a preface, "under various damaging conditions", and the greater part "in haste to catch late posts". Which is very characteristic of him, or used to be, for in those early days he would not even have aimed to catch such late posts if there had been any later. I never met him until after he came to London, and rely for what I know of him before then on the personal reminiscences scattered through "The Child in the Fields", "The Orange Idealist", and other of the essays in that first book of his.

If, when he was very young, he became an Orangeman, or, rather, an Orange boy, it was evidently owing to the influence of a benign but fiercely Protestant old nurse, "who believed in her heart that God was an Orangeman. She also believed that a strong family likeness existed between Satan and the Pope of Rome." She had the gentlest eyes behind black-rimmed glasses, and "her face was saintily sad under a bonnet rich in widow's bugles", but she had such a hatred of Roman Catholics that she would horrify him with stories of their wicked designs and gory details of the St. Bartholomew massacre, and taught him to worship King William III "as I am afraid I did not worship God". When the Twelfth of July was near, the great day for celebrating the Battle of the Boyne with processions through the town and wild riots between Protestants and Roman Catholics—

"On the eve of 'the Twelfth,' as it is called, she led me into the noisy country of the arches, and, taking me into a dark little shop, bought me a paper orange sash for a penny. In some years, when money was abundant, she provided me with a shilling drum as well: she never let a year pass without seeing that I had, at least, a tin whistle.

206

ROBERT LYND

She was an infectious propagandist. She was, for the time, a saint admitted to the splendours of Paradise, or— a better simile—a war-horse smelling the battle not too far off. As for me, she led me into every extravagance of enthusiasm."

As he stood in the street with her, watching the thousands of Orangemen march past with drums roaring and banners waving, he was an Orangeman himself, "at least in my beating pulses and along my quivering spine". But that was all left behind him far away and long ago when he arrived in London, and one would never have guessed then that he had once entertained such fiery and fanatical prejudices; for by then he had shed them and become the reasonable, tolerant, equable-minded citizen of the world who is revealed in his essays as one more amused than irritated by the follies, vanities, self-importances of mankind, who, seeing both sides of a question, can sympathise with hopes, ambitions, beliefs he does not share, has too keen a sense of the ridiculous ever to be oracular, but can lose his temper gloriously, and grow angry and bitter against manifest injustice to nations or to individuals, against wrongs done by the strong to those who have not the strength or the means to retaliate successfully. "The passion for justice", he says in one of his essays in "The Passion for Labour", "will outlive any statesman that God has yet created"; and it is the only passion, so far as I have seen, that ever breaks up the friendly quietude of his easy-going manner and rouses him to indignation.

Though he writes, or seems to write, freely and intimately of himself and his philosophy of life, conversationally he is in these matters one of the most reticent of men. If I said much of his ideals, or even of his love of Ireland, he would probably conclude, regretfully, that I was degenerating into a babbling sentimentalist; so I shall leave you to discover these from his "Home Life in Ireland" (1909); "Rambles in Ireland" (1912); "Ireland a Nation" (1919); and here and there from "Irish and English", and those other books of his essays that whimsically, fantastically, with a mellow or flippant humour, but in all seriousness, even when he is laughing at himself the while, tell you more about him than can be told by anyone else.

I might let myself describe him as gentle, only he would resent that as much as Lamb resented it when Coleridge applied that epithet to him. Moreover, it would be as misleading in his case as it was in Lamb's: he preserves a tranquil disposition, which is mistaken for gentleness, because he is indifferent to many of those things about which other folk are always ready to become excited and quarrelsome. In his essay "On Being Lord So–

and–So ", he remarks that the abolition of the House
of Lords is not one of his ruling passions; and if
one of his friends became a Bolshevist and another
a Fascist I am quite sure he would not cut either;
and if Professor Keith went to him and showed him
all the scientific evidence which proves that there
is no more soul in man than there is in a turnip, he
would listen patiently, perhaps laughing quietly at
intervals when any of the evidence tickled him,
but—unless he was short of a subject for his next
day's essay—he would not be stirred to write to the
papers about it, simply because he would feel that
if man had a soul he would not have to lose it to
verify a scientific opinion, and he would not wish
to spoil the Professor's enjoyment of his discovery.
He is contented to live and let live; his own views
are good enough for him, and he is willing to assume
that other men's views may be good enough for
them, and, except when he is frankly frivolous, or
playing with an odd or grotesque fancy, it is this
gracious spirit of reasonableness and common-sense
philosophy that are the charm and distinctive notes
of his essays.

Not long after he came to London, he was writing
for *To-Day*, that was edited then by Jerome's
successors, Frank Rutter and Ladbroke Black, and
contributing a weekly literary causerie to *Black and
White*, and in those literary causeries you find the

first sprightly runnings of that critical gift which
has reached a brilliant maturity since he has been
writing essays and criticisms for the *New Statesman*
and for the *Daily News*, of which for some years
past he has been literary editor.

No contemporary critic has a surer sense of
beauty, a more finely sensitive taste, and he brings
to the judgment of books the same sense of humour
and proportion, the same consistent, rational tolerance and wise reasonableness that he brings to the
judgment of men. At the close of his "Books and
Authors" is an essay on "The Critic" which, read
in its entirety, exemplifies the unruffled reasonableness and quiet strength and independence of
character in him that are carelessly mistaken for
gentleness.

"People often forget," he says, "that criticism, like poetry,
is of many kinds. The critics themselves are, perhaps the
worst transgressors in the matter. They are divided into
almost as many sects as the theologians, and every sect but
one regards its own standards as the very rules of salvation.
This would not matter so much if it did not lead to the
excommunication of all the critics who cannot subscribe to
the same creed. There is nothing more absurd in the
history of literature than the severities of the excommuni-
cating sort of critic. A critic has the right to condemn
any work, critical or other, which is bad of its kind. He
has not the right to say that only his own kind of criticism
is good. . . . The standards of sublunar critics are but
guesses. The critic who claims that they are more is simply
a dogmatist who climbs into a pulpit when he should be

going on a pilgrimage. . . . The critic must have respect
for the life of his own times as well as for the writings of
the dead. He cannot safely yield to the belief that great
literature is a temple that has already been built. If he
does not know that creation is still going on, he is little
more than a guide to the ruins of classical architecture."

There is the same urbane, humane philosophy,
as I say, in his judgment of men, as when, for
instance, in an essay on "Changes in Human
Nature" he lays it down that

"The German, the Frenchman, the Russian, the Italian,
the Irishman and the Jew are all both like and unlike the
Englishman. The mistake the hostile kind of Englishman
makes about them is in thinking that they are unlike him
in the ingredients of human nature, whereas they are unlike
him only in codes, conventions and circumstances. . . .
Most good statesmanship consists in knowing that your
enemy is like yourself, only worse."

That is the key-note in all these seventeen volumes
of his essays; their moods range from the delicacy
and wistful tenderness of such sketches and musings
as "The Little Angel", "The Empty House",
"The Country", "On Knowing the Difference",
to burlesque dissertations on "Hats", "Baths",
"The Money Lender"; from critical studies of
Keats, Poe, Henley, Max Beerbohm, to lively
accounts of cricket and football matches, boxing,
racing, and the mysteries of betting. Like Addison,
he finds his themes in contemporary life and

211

character, writes for and about his own day, often, no doubt, at the eleventh hour and against time for the next day's paper, sometimes on topics as frail as this year's leaves, but when these frailties are weeded out and the best of Lynd's many books condensed into one, it is my faith that, if Professor Keith is wrong and we can come back by-and-by to revisit the glimpses of the moon, we shall find that one book on the shelves of posterity, and a nearer neighbour there to Lamb than to Addison.

ARTHUR MACHEN

IT is many years since a famous Nonconformist divine, preaching on the common brotherhood of men, startled his congregation with the passionate pronouncement, "I will wear no clothes to distinguish myself from my fellow creatures!" On second thoughts, no doubt, they saw his meaning and approved of it. And there are moods in which I also can approve of that modest desire to be at one with the race, and not to cultivate an appearance of singularity which might suggest an exclusive dedication and seem to set a man apart from his kind. But there are moods in which I think otherwise—in which I feel a sort of regret that men "go into" literature and journalism now precisely as they go into stockbroking, accountancy, drapery or the frozen meat trade, treating the literary calling, in all its branches, strictly as a matter of business and becoming as business-like in habits and attire as the most practical money-making merchant of them all.

For it is not to be denied that this secularisation of the literary mind, with its sartorial effects on the literary body, is taking much of the romance out of life, and depriving the visible world of a good deal of its picturesqueness. Shaw, mainly because of his beard and long lean figure, Sir Hall Caine, also because of his beard, added to his wealth of hair, his large black hat and flowing cape, are almost our only authors, and Hannen Swaffer, because of his wild locks and lantern-jaws, his large black hat, flowing black tie and funereal suit, is almost our only journalist to-day who can be recognised anywhere at a glance. Arnold Bennett is clothed so beautifully in the fashion that he is often spoken of as "beau Bennett" and passes in Bond Street for one of the idle rich; Kipling, Wells and Galsworthy dress like ordinary men, and have no more hair than is worn by lawyers and military persons; the same being true of Alfred Noyes and John Masefield; of Walpole and Swinnerton; of Phillips Oppenheim and Edgar Wallace. Sala has described how published portraits had made everybody so familiar with the look of Dickens, his characteristic beard and flowing hair, that wherever he took his walks abroad he was continually being identified by passers-by, many of whom would turn and excitedly point him out to others; but I have often seen Barrie in the Strand, in a commonplace jacket suit and a bowler, quietly strolling through the crowd with his hands behind his back, nothing in the least sensational or unusual about him, and have never seen anybody show a sign of knowing who he was.

It used not to be so. Fleet Street and the Strand were not always given over to pedestrians of the dull uniformity of pattern that is appropriate and proper in Lothbury and London Wall. There was a time when you could not walk from Ludgate Hill to Charing Cross without meeting a dozen men who allowed their individualities to find expression in their outward aspects, so that, even if you did not know them personally, you knew that, anyhow, they were authors or journalists, and the knowledge thrilled you pleasantly and brought a touch of colour into the monotony of the scene. But the change was beginning to come even before the war. Stanley Portal Hyatt (and if you have not read the best of his novels, particularly "Little Brown Brother", you have missed some good books) was the most unconventional of men; he had roughed it in the wilds of South Africa, and after his return to civilisation was never comfortable anywhere in anything but a cloth cap and an easy old tweed suit. Nevertheless, he told me, in his latter days, it had been borne in upon him that if you wished to do good business and put up your prices you must impress editors and publishers with a notion that you were practical and prosperous, and that you could not do this unless you always called on them well dressed and wearing a top hat. He was so convinced of this, but so ashamed to be seen out in such raiment, that when he came to town from his home out by Amersham Common he would bring a stiff collar, a black morning coat and waistcoat and black trousers in a bag, and kept a beautiful top hat in his locker at the Press Club. There he would go to put the loathed garments on, and there he would go to take them off again before he went home; and I have seen him, in between those operations, lounging along Fleet Street, attired for conquest, and never felt sure that editors and publishers would regard his figure as impressive. For his was a lank and awkward shape; the top hat should have been a size larger; the coat was short in the sleeves and revealed nearly all the white cuffs he had, and the trousers were braced so vigorously that they scarcely reached to his boots. I have stopped him in such circumstances to inquire how the campaign was progressing, and though he used words about his costume which I will not repeat, nothing ever shook his faith in its grandeur and efficacy.

But if much has been taken a little still abides. On rare occasions the drab sameness of the Fleet Street crowd will be relieved for you by a glimpse of Chesterton who, at least in this matter of personal appearance, remains a breezy and independent nonconformist; or Hamlin Garland, over from the States and looking remarkably like Nathaniel Hawthorne; or the author of the Socialist national anthem, "The Red Flag", with his huge white moustache, his flaming scarlet tie, and a black felt hat with such an ample brim as I have seen on no other hat except the one worn by Ellis Roberts, who also maintains, in these particulars, the picturesque old traditions of the street he too seldom visits; or you may see Arthur Machen.

Years back, when he became for a time a working journalist (and journalism rarely gets so fine a literary artist into her service) you might run across him any day of the week at Ludgate Circus, in Fleet Street and the purlieus of Whitefriars, and his very unlikeness to the multitude round about him gave you a feeling that he belonged there, that he was native to the place, while the others would have seemed as much or more at home in any other street of the city. His sturdy form and gait are vaguely reminiscent of Dr. Johnson, but, instead of a wig, from under his small felt hat his thick iron-grey hair streams down stiff as wire and is cut off straight at his shoulders after a style of toilet that prevailed among mediæval Venetian senators. To set eyes on him thus, especially if the weather was not too mild for him to be enveloped in his great cape-overcoat, warmed you with a feeling that life had not yet been reduced quite to a dead level, that the free Bohemian spirit which quickened the world of literature in its golden age was not yet extinct, nor the glorious individuality of Fleet Street wholly departed from it.

In days before the war, and before he had adventured into daily journalism, you might find Machen now and then of evenings paying a visit to a delightfully informal little club (poor Richard Middleton was one of its members) that met in a room over a tavern in Buckingham Street, Strand, a genial, friendly presence, smoking a comfortable pipe, a tankard of ale on the table beside him, joining in the talk, from time to time, in that slow, deep voice of his, with the same quiet humour or quaint fantasy of thought and phrase he uses so magically in his books. Nor was he a stranger in those far off times to another unorthodox little club—a club of a dozen or so young writers who met periodically in a wine cellar in Queen Street, Cheapside, the vintner himself being a poet of no mean quality; an exclusive little club to which a new member was only admitted after he had subscribed to an elaborate, grotesquely solemn ritual which was prepared by Arthur Edward Waite, who rejoiced in ornate ceremonial, and has been named by no less an authority than Monsignor William Barry one of the most brilliantly intellectual of English mystics.

ARTHUR MACHEN

The war put an end to nearly all those friendly, odd, Bohemian clubs that used to be plentiful in London, but have now been replaced by night clubs where you go in seemly evening-dress to jazz and not to talk. There is one small survivor of such pre-war symposia to which Machen now and then makes his way; otherwise he satisfies his unpretentious social instinct by holding informal gatherings of his English and American friends at his home in St. John's Wood.

No doubt he has a good deal in common with that Hermit of his own "Hieroglyphics", who was a visionary, a mystic, with "an esoteric philosophy of things", one for whom "Art in general and the art of literature in particular had a very high significance and interest". But, unlike the Hermit, his love of solitude is not unleavened, and if he is more at home among what is left of the genial amenities of our literary Bohemia than among the frosty etiquettes of polite society it is because he is not merely gregarious but, when the mood comes to him, profoundly sociable. Withal, he is almost as lonely a figure in our world of letters as Donne, Sir Thomas Browne and Beddoes were in theirs, and he has close affinities with the first two in his religious mysticism, and with all three in his sense of the terror and mystery and spiritual beauty that enfold and are enfolded by the life of man and clothe even the simplicities and commonplaces of his everyday environment with wonder and occult significance. "I am a desirer of mysteries and unknown things", he has said, and these reveal themselves to him in the drab streets and dreariest suburbs of London as they did by the "grey and silvery river" and the eerie dark forest of the place where he was born.

He was born in Monmouthshire, in the small, ancient town of Caerleon-on-Usk, with its memories of Roman occupation and its more glamorous memories of the half-mythical King Arthur, the remains of whose Round Table still survive there. His father was a clergyman, and "Far-Off Things", in which Machen has written his autobiography, tells you how potently his mind and work have been influenced by the poetry of old romance that belonged to his early surroundings. "The older I grow," he says, "the more firmly am I convinced that anything which I may have accomplished in literature is due to the fact that when my eyes were first opened in earliest childhood they had before them the vision of an enchanted land. . . . Solitude and woods and deep lanes and wonder; these were the chief elements of my life . . . and the run of a thoroughly ill-selected library." But he bought for himself, if they were not in the library, De Quincey's "Opium Eater" and "Don Quixote",

the "Arabian Nights" and the romances of Scott
which he read with great joy, "curled up in odd
corners of the rectory . . . curled up and en-
tranced so that I was deaf, and gave no answer
when they called to me".

Before he was twenty he came to London with
the idea of passing examinations and making medicine
his profession, but did not go through with that.
Presently he was making a meagre livelihood as a
publisher's assistant; then by taking a few pupils;
living sparely in a garret: reading incessantly and
writing poetry. He spent his leisure in tramping
all about London, "a shabby, sorry figure; and
always alone". When neither by writing nor otherwise he could keep the wolf from the door, he
returned home for a while; but came back to London
to a drudgery of cataloguing books and to writing
as a free-lance, and for an interval, when he was
nearing forty, he became an actor in the Benson
Company.

Meanwhile, in the opening years of this century
he had started publishing books. His first, "The
Anatomy of Tobacco", he has described as "a grave
burlesque of what I loved"; this and "The Chronicle
of Clemendy" were interesting forerunners of the
three books, "The Great God Pan", "The Three
Imposters", and "The Hill of Dreams", which
satisfied the discerning that a new planet had swum

into their ken, a writer of strange, original genius whose subtle imaginative gifts wrought in horror and mystery and fantasy with all the potency of Poe but to different purposes and with a finer sense of beauty and whimsical humour than belonged to Poe, as a story-teller. In those three books, and in "The House of Souls", "The Terror", "The Secret Glory", "Far Off Things", "Things Far and Near", "Dog and Duck", and "Hieroglyphics" (a delightfully discursive, shrewdly critical and provocative series of talks on books and authors and of the touchstone which proves what is great in literature) are, I think, the highest, most significant things as teller of tales and as essayist that Machen has done. Round these, as large or lesser stars round a moon, I would rank his "War and the Christian Faith", "The Return", "The Bowmen", "Strange Roads", "The London Adventure", "Ornaments in Jade", "The Canning Wonder", "Dreads and Drolls". I have not read "The Shining Pyramid" (which contains, I believe, miscellaneous writings of his that were collected by an American enthusiast), and "Dr. Stiggins", a laboured satire on a famous nonconformist minister, seems to me his one failure.

But although Machen's genius was recognised over twenty years ago success, commercially speaking, was much slower in coming to him, or, I take it, he would not have been lured on to the staff of a great daily. It was then (during the war) that he wrote a vivid little fantasy of the angels of Mons, which took such hold on the public imagination that before long it was passing current as true; soldiers testified to having seen those phantom shapes in the battle; and Machen's circumstantial account of the whole thing in "The Bowman" has not even yet persuaded everybody that it was nothing but fiction. Whether the notoriety of this story, or his graphic descriptive accounts of public events in the newspaper, helped to bring him into vogue I do not know. But since the war he has come into his own. A uniform edition of his works has been published by Secker; collectors are paying amazing prices for his first editions, and a Machen cult has sprung up and is flourishing, especially in America. A year ago, a Chicago bookseller, visiting my office, confessed that his chief aim in London was to see Arthur Machen, but he had no introductions to him and was afraid to call. "Some of us in my country," he said, "are just mad over Machen. There's a group of young writers, poets and critics, who meet at times in a room behind my shop—they've studied and lectured and written about him, and I wouldn't care to go back and tell them I haven't seen him." I gave him my word Machen was not the forbidding recluse he fancied, and that a friendly request from an American would bring him an appointment. "Well," said he, going away, "I'll write that letter, and if it fails, you'll see me again, and I'll get an introduction to him from somebody if I have to go down on my knees for it." As Keats wrote after visiting Burns' cottage, "Oh, smile among the gods, for this is fame!"

ARCHIBALD MARSHALL

ARCHIBALD MARSHALL

MANY years ago I picked up on a bookstall a second-hand copy of Charles Lever's "Sir Brook Fosbrooke". I had not heard of the book before, and bought it out of nothing but a tepid curiosity, for my early delight in Lever's high-spirited, riotous stories was by then somewhat cooled. But Sir Brook took me by surprise, and revived my interest in its author; it was so unlike the novels that made him famous; so unlike, and so much better, that to me it seems the best of all his books, not only in form and style, but in its truth to life and character. Soon after I had read it I chanced to call on Edmund Downey (whose publishing house of Ward & Downey then flourished in York Street, Covent Garden), and found him busy with the proofs of his noble edition of Lever's complete works, and being newly enthusiastic over my discovery, I opened it to him. "Of course I've included 'Sir Brook Fosbrook'. It is one of the least known of Lever's novels—I seldom meet anybody who has even heard of it—but I agree with you," he said "that it is about the best he ever did."

225

THE GLORY THAT WAS GRUB STREET

Which is a parable, whose bearings, as Captain Cuttle would say, lie in the application of it. You can never be sure you know an author if you know only the work that has made him popular; and, in general, the ablest and most interesting novels are not necessarily those that make the most noise. Lever had so thoroughly established himself as an author of the noisier kind of novel that when, in his last years, he brought out this very quiet one it barely succeeded in making itself heard. It would have had no better chance of a hearing if it had made its first appearance to-day; for we are all speeded up now, living at high pressure, with no palate but for highly-seasoned pleasures, so that, to suit our post-war temperaments, our very fiction must be an excitement, a quick debauch instead of a gracious recreation. If "Cranford" were one of this year's new books I don't believe it would sell a thousand copies. If "The Vicar of Wakefield" had been written yesterday, no Dr. Johnson could persuade any publisher to pay Goldsmith fifty pounds for it to-morrow. The engine has superseded the horse, we fly on wheels or in the air, and among all the social and political changes and distractions that have broken up the easy current of public life we cannot capture a mood that is sufficiently tranquil to give the unaggressive charm of such stories a chance to take hold upon us.

226

ARCHIBALD MARSHALL

Therefore it is surprising that the novels of
Archibald Marshall have come into favour in this
country and in America, and not surprising that,
even so, they fall short of obtaining all the popularity
they deserve. For though Marshall is one of the
ablest and most interesting of contemporary novelists,
he is as truthfully and quietly realistic as Trollope;
he does not tittilate a jaded pleasure-seeker with
bizarre or startling plots, or with studies of psychological freaks; the men and women of his tales are
not abnormally afflicted with sexual obsessions, but
are very natural, reasonable, decent human creatures
who have not qualified for a side-show or a museum
but are such as you may meet almost any day at
large in the flesh. If his psychology were less subtle,
more obvious, more superficial, he would have been
labelled as an acute psychologist before now; but he
rightly presents his creations with their works inside
them and reveals their mental and moral promptings in talk and action, for he is a born novelist,
an authentic teller of stories; and the stories he
tells are very natural stories whose incidents and
events build up the characters and fill the lives of
his very natural people—who are, for the most part,
country squires, lords of the manor, their families,
friends, dependents, the local gentry and humbler
members of rural communities—that play prominent
or minor parts in his everyday comedies and tragedies.

THE GLORY THAT WAS GRUB STREET

There has been no truer historian of certain phases of English life that are gradually passing away; and if he makes you aware of the comfort and dignity and kindliness that were associated with the old order, he brings home to you the pathos and drama of the struggle between the traditional lords of the soil, who are not fitted to cope with modern conditions, and the newly rich who are forcing their way in among them, contesting their ancient privileges, or lavishly buying them out and supplanting them. And though he loves the serene dignities and exclusive social code of a decaying aristocracy, he is alive to the virtues of the self-made invaders, and is equally faithful in his presentation of them.

When Yale University conferred its degree of LL.D. on Archibald Marshall in 1921 it stated on its diploma, as reason for honouring him: "He has so held up the mirror to the life and manners of his own countrymen that we across the sea know and love them". He is far from being without honour in his own country, but he has found a larger public, a more generous measure of appreciation in America than here. I am not sure, however, that they are right who say America was first to give due recognition to the easy strength, the sound literary quality and realistic truthfulness of his work. I read his "Exton Manor" when it was published in 1907 and remember with what a chorus of praise it was received by English reviewers. It was much the finest of his first four books; he had completely found himself in that and mastered his method, and has only surpassed it in fullness of narrative power and subtlety and variety of characterisation in the "Clinton" series of novels and in the still later three volumes of the "Anthony Dare" series. But while in this country we may claim credit for ranking him without undue delay among our chief living novelists, it was America that brought him into vogue, and made such a stir about him on the other side of the Atlantic as had the effect of increasing his popularity over here. And I fancy Professor William Lyon Phelps was mainly responsible for this.

Professor Phelps has told how in 1915, when Marshall had twelve books to his name, he came across the then newly-published "Rank and Riches", the fourth of the "Clinton" series. "So long as I live," he wrote, "it will hold a secure place in my heart, for this is the first work of the author's that I saw. Indeed, I had never heard of him until I picked up 'Rank and Riches'. I started to read it with no conception of the keen delight in store; after finishing it I wrote to the publishers, 'Who on earth is Archibald Marshall? There is no one like him in the world. Send me everything he has written'. Since that moment of exaltation I have read and re-read the Clinton books, and each time they seem better."

In his own more subdued way Marshall makes you as familiar with his characters as Dickens makes you with his. They are so vitally yet unexaggeratedly real that you might be forgiven for suspecting he made a practice of drawing them from actual persons. I believe he only once succumbed to temptation and did this, but all the rest of them, high and low, major and minor, are as minutely and convincingly realised as if he had never done anything else.

He came to this close, sympathetic knowledge of country life and conditions largely by living in such surroundings as he pictures; but he has lived much in cities and travelled a good deal, and has drawn on these experiences also. After leaving Trinity College, Cambridge, he went for a while into a City office and was to have qualified for partnership in his father's business, but turned aside from that career to study for the Church, and, though he did not take Holy Orders, his leaning to that vocation may to some extent account for the interest his novels show in clerical affairs, and his varied and brilliant studies of rectors, vicars and curates and their wives.

When his first novel was published he had turned thirty, and "Peter Binney: Undergraduate" was not an auspicious beginning. It was mildly amusing, readable, and had touches of humour, but, except in the presentation of Peter's father, was not much of a shadow to be cast before the greater novels that were coming after it. His second, "The House of Merrilees", showed a notable advance on this; with a somewhat Dickensian plot of mystery and melodrama, it has not a little of the restraint and grace of style which are native to his maturer work. This novel wandered about London for three or four years and was rejected everywhere until, setting up as a publisher in the firm of Alston Rivers, he published it himself in 1905. A year later, in "Richard Baldock", a dramatic and powerful story of the conflicting temperaments of a father and son, he had left his 'prentice days behind him and achieved something that went beyond all that his earlier books had promised and quite definitely placed him as an author capable of work more enduring than that in the average book of the week.

Having abandoned publishing, he became editor of the *Daily Mail* "Books Supplement"; then for a few years acted as its special correspondent, and as such visited America and Australia, the latter journey having its record in his sketches of travel, "Sunny Australia". Meanwhile, he had published "Exton Manor" (1907), "Many Junes" (1908), and the two first of the "Clinton" volumes—"The Squire's Daughter" (1909) and "The Eldest Son" (1911).

Somewhere about this time he gave up journalism to devote himself entirely to the writing of fiction, as he has done ever since, except that during the War he served as Paris Correspondent of the *Daily News*.

Two novels, beside "Peter Binney", stand outside what may be called the Archibald Marshall canon: "Upsidonia"—in which, actuated by the knowledge that

> "Hearts just as pure and fair
> May beat in Belgrave Square
> As in the lowly air
> Of Seven Dials,"

he burlesqued and satirised the apparent notion of extravagant humanitarians that wealth and birth are sins to be avoided and poverty a virtue to be cultivated—"Upsidonia" is one of them, and the other is "The Mystery of Redmarsh Farm", a real, all-wool, double-breasted sensational yarn of the most thrilling description; and I reminded Marshall of this when he told me he did not naturally see life in terms of stories and protested that he had no gift for constructing plots. "Yes, but I did not invent the plot of 'Redmarsh Farm", said he; "it was given to me by Lord Northcliffe. He wanted me to write a serial for the *Daily Mail*, and when I told him such fiction was out of my line, he was still insistent and undertook to furnish me with a plot. He did so, and I wrote the story around it with modifications and additions—necessarily; for the serial began to appear as soon as a few chapters were ready and proved so successful with the *Mail's* readers that I was urged not to end it too quickly, and it went on till it had run to four hundred thousand words." It was condensed for re-publication, and was as successful in a book as it had been in the newspaper. But having thus demonstrated that he could do this sort of thing triumphantly, he let some fourteen years pass before he was moved to do it again, and then, in collaboration with H. A. Vachell, produced in 1925 that story of plot and sensation, "Mr. Allen".

In the interval Archibald Marshall had gone on in his quieter fashion writing the concluding volumes of the "Clinton" series and, among others, such admirable novels as "Roding Rectory" (which contains, in Dr. Merrow, the finest of all his clerical characters), "Abingdon Abbey" and "The Graftons", "The Hall and the Grange", and, to repeat myself, he has gone a touch beyond any of these in the "Anthony Dare" trilogy. "Anthony Dare", "The Education of Anthony Dare", and "The Progress of Anthony Dare". More recently we have had from him the lighter, entertaining chronicles of "The Allbright Family".

Without resorting to unusual mysteries, lurid incidents or melodramatic surprises, Marshall has

233

an extraordinary power of creating a cumulative interest in his stories and their people; he can heighten that interest with excitements, such as the baffling jewel robbery in "The Honour of the Clintons", but he does not use this episode as a sensational novelist would. The crowning importance of the robbery lies in its effect upon the conduct of Squire Clinton, in whether the traditions of his race, his high sense of honour will enable him to rise above the temptation to avoid disgrace to one of his family by submitting to blackmail, and you become as intensely absorbed in his ethical dilemma as you could be in any romance of crime or mystery.

That is the magic of Archibald Marshall's art. With a sure knowledge of humanity and an unpretentious, imaginative cunning, he so draws his characters that he wins your understanding and your sympathy for whatever concerns them and, without need for wild alarms and excursions, keeps you closely and increasingly interested in the intimate annals of such men and women as do in fact make the majority of the population of the world we ourselves inhabit. If his vicar's wife, Mrs. Prentice, in "Exton Manor", is mischievous, snobbish, tuft-hunting, on the other hand, Lady Ruth, of "Roding Rectory", is a parson's wife of a charming and wholly different type. His young people are as varied and exactly realistic as are their elders, and there are always more likeable than unlikeable people living in his pages. His occasional villains and undesirables are not over-emphasised; he consistently sets things down as they are, simply because they happen to be so; and it is this uncompromising lifelikeness that is the distinctive quality of his work.

CHRISTOPHER MORLEY

CHRISTOPHER MORLEY

I⊤ has been said often enough—I have said it often
enough myself—and it must be true since it has
been said so often, that it is as unfortunate for an
author to be versatile as it is for a man to be born
with three heads. With such a superfluity of
natural gifts he may win notoriety and some money
as a freak in a side-show, but he can hardly hope
to succeed in getting himself taken so seriously that
the management will put his variety entertainment
in large type at the top of the bill as the great star
turn in the exhibition. In spite of the proverb, it
is found in practice that even two heads are not
better than one, and there can be no doubt whatever that more than two amount to a catastrophe.
A wise man, finding himself thus endowed and
ambitious to rise and be received in the best and
highest circles, will concentrate on one and, at all
risks, amputate the others.

The versatile author is faced with the same
problem. People in general may talk as if they
admired an Admirable Crichton, but in their hearts
they distrust him; he rather bewilders them, and

they are much likelier to excuse themselves from following him by putting him aside as a jack-of-all-trades. For of course he is difficult to follow, and only the enterprising minority, whose tastes are sufficiently catholic, care to keep track of him. Instead of going steadily ahead, always along the same road, he is continually making excursions into byways, and if he cannot break himself of this habit, before it is too late, decide what goal he wants to reach and go straight for it, he usually ends by leaving most of his followers lost in those different byways and arriving nowhere in particular, at last, with nobody much at his heels.

I am not suggesting that this is going to be the awful fate of Christopher Morley; it might have been; but there are clear signs that he has so far only been feeling industriously around to find himself and the way he ought to travel; and that he has found them. As Hugh Walpole says in a preface to "Thunder on the Left", Morley's gifts "were as many as they were dangerous, and that especial danger of finding life too enchanting to be true is difficult to escape because it becomes so easily a habit". He has been described to me—unhappily I have never met him—as a big, genial, friendly man, with an intense interest and joy in life; "a fellow of infinite jest" and fantasy, but one who is a tremendous worker and brings a fresh enthusiasm

to every sort of work he is moved to do. You could
not read much that he has written without guessing
at something of this; you would guess from its
glancing alertness and sense of spontaneity, that even
if some of it had been done as part of a journalist's
regular job, he had put his heart as well as his mind
into it and found pleasure in the doing; you would
guess he had been having a good time, letting his
fancy and imagination range at large, catching at
every kind of idea they brought home to him and
carelessly embodying each in its different, appropriate medium, because he happens to have a breadth
and brilliance of capacity which enabled him to do
so. As a result, counting two written in collaboration, he has in the last sixteen years published five-
and-twenty books of poems, serious and humorous,
short stories, sketches, essays, novels, skits, and a
few plays. His wildest burlesque and the most
thoughtful and restrained of his poems, essays,
stories have often been touched with a characteristic
fantasy, whimsical, satirical or graciously tender,
that has brought them into an elusive harmony;
otherwise he has been a very Proteus in the various
forms he has used. That is the real way how to
be happy though literary, but, for the reasons suggested, it is not the way to a stable popularity, nor a
sure way, as a substitute for concentration, in which
an author can develop the greatest of his gifts. And

239

you may depend that Morley knows this, for it looks as if he were beginning to act accordingly.

He was born in 1890, at Haverford, Pennsylvania, and, having graduated at Haverford College, went as a Rhodes Scholar to Oxford, from 1910 to 1913. While he was still at Oxford, in 1912, his first book, a book of poems, "The Eighth Sin", was published by B. H. Blackwell, the well-known publisher of that city. He returned to America, and for five years was on the editorial staff of the great publishing house of Doubleday, Page & Co. Then he took to journalism, and was successively associated with the *Ladies' Home Journal*, *Philadelphia Public Ledger*, the New York *Evening Post* (to which he began to contribute his lively column, "The Bowling Green", in 1920), and the *Saturday Review of Literature*.

Meanwhile, in 1917, appeared his first prose fiction, "Parnassus on Wheels" and a second volume of poems "Songs from a Little House". In 1918 came a collection of his essays, "Shandygaff"; next year, more poems, "The Rocking Horse", more fiction, "The Haunted Bookshop", a skit on prohibition, "In the Sweet Dry and Dry", and another book of essays, "Mince Pie". That was a year of plenty, and 1920 rivalled it, with the sketches and essays, "Travels in Philadelphia", a story, "Kathleen", "Pipefuls", another book of essays, and "Hide and Seek", which contains some of the best poems of his that I have read. It contains, for instance, that sonnet, "In An Auction Room", touching with a wry humour and poignance on the sale of Keats's love letters, and closing with the ironic comment:

> "Song that outgrew the singer! Bitter love
> That broke the proud hot heart it held in thrall.
> Poor script, where still those tragic passions move—
> *Eight hundred bid: fair warning: the last call:*
> The soul of Adonais, like a star. . . .
> *Sold for eight hundred dollars—Doctor R.!*"

The next year (1921) brought a further three books, "Tales from a Rolltop Desk", "Plum Pudding" (essays), and another collection of his poems, "Chimneysmoke". If, as a poet, Morley's place is on the lower slopes of Parnassus, there is the individual note and the same charm of fancy and sentiment in a good deal of his verse that you find in his prose, breaking in there at times on his drollest and most irresponsible moods. Very characteristic of him are the lines "To a Post-Office Inkwell" (in "Chimneysmoke"), characteristic of his insight of the homely beauty and significance that is in common, everyday things:

> "How many humble hearts have dipped
> In you, and scrawled their manuscript!
> Have shared their secrets, told their cares,
> Their curious and quaint affairs!

241

THE GLORY THAT WAS GRUB STREET

Your pool of ink, your scratchy pen,
Have moved the lives of unborn men,
And watched young people, breathing hard,
Put Heaven on a postal card."

A later book of verse, "Translations from the
Chinese" (1922) is in a very different vein, as you
may gather from the fact that the verses are translations of such Celestial poets as No Sho and Mu
Kow, and that Morley confesses his sole knowledge
of Chinese was derived from laundry slips. To
summarise the remainder of my catalogue, between
1922 and to-day we have had from him, in collaboration with Don Marquis, "Pandora Lifts the Lid";
we have had "The Arrow", four volumes of essays,
"The Powder of Sympathy", "Inward Ho!"
"Religio Journalistici", and as delightful a miscellany of travel and general sketches as any he has
done, "The Romany Stain", a one-act play,
"Rehearsal", and his two latest collections of poems,
"Parsons' Pleasure", and "Toulemonde". In
addition, for like Browning's careful host I have
left the finest wine till last, there are "Where the
Blue Begins" (1922) and "Thunder on the Left"
(1926).

With "Where the Blue Begins" Morley seemed,
at one stride, to pass his Rubicon and stand among
authors who are to be taken seriously. Until then,
I suppose, he was looked upon by many of us rather

242

as a clever trifler, a brilliant journalist and miscellaneous writer whose multifarious work suggested that he had greater gifts than he had yet realised or exerted himself to employ. That was, I am afraid, our notion of him over here, though they knew him better and he had a considerable vogue in his own country. But when we read "Where the Blue Begins" we woke up to a recognition of its strange power and originality, and to the fact that he had suddenly outrivalled himself. It is a novel, but not of the orthodox pattern; it would be more at home bracketed with "Gulliver's Travels"; for it is a blend of allegory, fantasy, satire, fable, poetry and philosophy. It is a story of Gissing, the dog, who lives in a world of dogs, where the animals think and talk and act much as if they were human beings. Gissing seeks for the meaning of life, as men do, broods on religion, is sceptical of its teachings and tries to find God in the world. After a splendidly successful interlude as a dog of business, he enters the Church as a lay reader, and moved one Sunday to exceed his authority mounts the pulpit and preaching of the mystery of Godhead tells his audience their idea of Him and of serving Him with trivial ceremony and ritual is all "on too petty a scale", and urges them to believe "it is even possible God may be a biped". Whereupon all the dogs in the congregation, led by a canine

Bishop, rise in such a howling of indignant fury that he is compelled to flee for safety. He escapes to the sea and gets aboard a ship as a stowaway. Here, having won the confidence of the captain, he soon contrives, by means of a ruse, to scare the crew and passengers into going off in the boats, and he sails on alone, an erratic and uncharted course, which brings him finally to unknown land. He goes ashore, and after some wandering, comes upon a ragged tramp seated by a fire in a thicket, and at this unwonted sight of a man he quivers with emotion, goes forward with feelings of joy and worship, to nestle his head contentedly on the vagrant's knee, satisfied that he has at last found God. Presently, he runs off reluctantly to see that the ship is safely moored, and discovers it dwindled to a toy boat and the vast ocean to nothing but the lake near his own house.

Like all allegory it is not always easy of comprehension; it is full of spiritual suggestion, here and there it is susceptible of more than one interpretation, and will probably mean different things to different readers. You can enjoy the wit and satire and the oddly fantastic story of it for their own sakes, but its covert parody of human life, thought and practice gives it a deeper interest and the inner significances you glimpse in mystical poems and parables.

244

Somewhat of this is true also of "Thunder on the Left", which is too well known by now for it to be necessary for me to attempt anything much of a summary. Briefly, it is a tale of a party of children gathered to celebrate the tenth birthday of one of them, Martin. They talk of their elders, of whether grown-ups are really happy and how impossible it is to find out, because if you question them they will never tell you things. They decide that they will, as a new kind of game, get into the country of the grown-ups as spies on them, and then "bring in a report". In blowing out the birthday candles each child has one wish, and as a consequence of Martin's wish the second chapter opens with the story of George Granville and his wife, Phyllis. With the development of the story other children of the birthday party take part in it, but, like Phyllis, they have arrived at years of maturity. In due course comes Martin himself, grown to manhood but still a boy in mind, and it dawns upon you, after a while, that Martin is, in fact also George, and that in his own name he is only there as the boy-spy. The experiences of these people who have projected themselves into the future and are living the lives that may be theirs in twenty years' time are subtly and suggestively handled. They seem real, but have an occasional consciousness of their unreality; there is an elusive

air of gramarye about it all, but the men and women
are very human in their emotions and their relations
with one another, and have gone through enough
to know that everything is not easy for their elders,
before it all fades like a dream and they are back
at the party which is just breaking up, and Martin,
at least, has some memory of what has passed.
Here, again, you may not always be sure in every
detail of exactly what Morley intends to convey,
but the meaning of the fantasy as a whole is so clear
that even he who runs can read it. There is wit
and worldly wisdom and whimsical satire in this
as in "Where the Blue Begins", and the humour
is so rarely strained or thin that such passing flaws
count for no more against the charm and skill of
these two remarkable books than do spots on the
sun. A dramatic version of "Thunder on the
Left" has been as successful as the novel. Morley
has been compared with Barrie; I think a comparison with Chesterton might be truer; but he is
so little like and so much unlike both it is futile
to compare him with either.

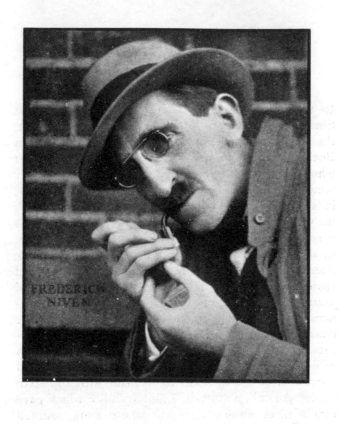

FREDERICK
NIVEN

FREDERICK NIVEN

In those pleasant days before the War to which at times one looks back rather wistfully, Robert Frost, the American poet, was living at Beaconsfield, in Buckinghamshire. He was not known as a poet when he arrived here, and though he was promptly recognised as one when he published in this country, in 1913, his first book of poems, "A Boy's Will", he was not trying to live by poetry then but was very practically engaged in farming. At that date, in the same county and not far from Beaconsfield, Frederick Niven was living, at Amersham, and sedulously earning his bread by literature and journalism. By 1913, to say nothing of his journalism, Niven had published six novels and one book of short stories; he scored an immediate success with the first of these, "Lost Cabin Mine", a brilliant romance of the Wild West, and proved himself an artist in homelier realism with the sixth "Ellen Adair", a story of Edinburgh life which gave him a place among novelists whose work counted for something as literature.

I have linked Frost and Niven together for no better reason than that they were comparative neighbours, and are linked in my mind because I happened to meet both about the same time. I don't believe they knew each other, but anyone who knew them might take a walk down Fleet Street at that time and by happy chance meet either of them taking a day in town to attend some literary function or pay business calls on editors and publishers. It was not long before Frost went home again to settle down and win fame in America. And it was not long before Niven, as he has himself written, "told my wife about British Columbia till we both got so that we had to go and look at it. Where the money came from I forget. I know that after we returned to London I once went out with her to see if an article I had sent to some paper had appeared, and on the way to the news-stand said, 'Oh, by the way, have you got the penny?'"

My memory is not clear about the exact years when these things occurred, but they had not been back more than a year or so when the lure of British Columbia proved too much for them again and Niven and his wife dropped in at my office one day to say good-bye and tell me they were off to the West once more. I gathered that they were only going on a visit, but might be away some time. The years have lengthened to seven or eight and they are still away, and it begins to look as if he were so much happier in that freer, less conventional

FREDERICK NIVEN

life among forests and mountains that were familiar
to him in his youth than in the tumult and strife
of London and its coteries that he intends to make
Nelson, B.C. his permanent address.

Though he was born at Valparaiso, Chili, in 1878,
Niven's people were Glasgow people, and he was
educated there, attended the Glasgow School of
Art, and was for two years assistant librarian at the
Glasgow Public Library. Then, while he was still
in his 'teens, he went West, and his experiences out
there supplied him with much of the material for
"Lost Cabin Mine", "Hands Up!" and other
romances; and in a more recent book, "Wild Honey",
he has written something in the way of an autobiographical account of those early years. He has
probably taken the historical novelist's licence with
facts and heightened an effect here and there or
added a touch or two to give force or completeness
to a dramatic incident, but though the story is
mainly about his two companions Hank and Sim,
and though at the outset he says that, in writing
"Wild Honey", he "had no desire whatever that
it should be looked upon as a portion of autobiography. I am not the protagonist, but the on-
looker, the reporter", a little farther on he assures
us that "the story I tell is not a hybrid of fact
and fiction but a narration of actual experience"
Anyhow, it squares with all he has told me of

those days of his youth, and begins with a sort of apologia:

"I came to Penny's Pit, high in the Dry Belt of British Columbia, simply because I was young and wanted to see the West, and did not want to see it only from a car window. I was not, in the accepted sense an immigrant. I was not a 'prospective settler.' I was just a wanderer, curiously looking at the world and encountering men I could never have met in my decorous home. As I had no trade, when I had to replenish my pocketbook (being also not a remittance man) I had to join the ranks of the unskilled labourers. . . . I took the job at Penny's Pit because it was in the open air, and because I wanted money to buy undervests and socks, and to pay my way somewhere else, and for my food when looking at that somewhere else, wherever it might be."

At sight, when I knew him, you would take him for a scholar and a dreamer; he walked with a stoop, and there was nothing in his tall, slight figure, his soft, hesitant voice and shy reserve of manner to indicate that he had ever been anything in the nature of a cow-puncher and a navvy; but out there at Penny's Pit he was one of an Extra Gang working on the Canadian Pacific Railway, his work being the "shovelling gravel out of a hillside into dump-carts that took it away to fill in gulches under trestle bridges". The place where he was so engaged was about half-way between Ashcroft and Kamloops on the main line of that railway. When they were not doing a little occasional work, his two companions

FREDERICK NIVEN

Hank and Sim were typical hoboes, a curious, quaint pair, and they and their adventures, their shrewd philosophy of life, all the best and the worst of them are preserved in "Wild Honey", for Niven not only worked beside them, he tramped with them, camped with them, picked up odd jobs, as they did, starved and rejoiced with them, and, having had his fill of such wanderings, went back to Scotland and wrote some of his memories into a dozen sketches which were published in the *Glasgow Weekly Herald*.

Then, after getting on to the staff of a Scottish paper, doing well as leader writer, and assistant fiction editor, he came to London (the only detail in which he has acted like an orthodox Scotsman) to do some editing here and contribute essays and poems to the *Daily News* and the *Nation*. And here he wrote that first novel, "Lost Cabin Mine", and from what I recollect of the praise it received from reviewers and the general stir it made, I should have said it was as auspicious a beginning as any young novelist could have desired, but he himself seems to deprecate that, for he has written, "When I sold it for . . . Oh, dear, Oh, dear! . . . draw a veil . . . !" All the same, if it did not put much in his purse, it launched him well on his literary career. The book was alive; there was a sort of morning freshness and vigour in it; you

251

felt that here was a man who had lived and had learned in living what he was telling in story.

Two years later, in his second novel, "An Island Providence", (1910) he was still roving on the shores of romance, but had given his imagination free reign, and was back in the seventeenth century with a glamorous, grimly realistic story of buca- neering that carries you from Devonshire to the Indies and cunningly recaptures the atmosphere and character of the period. This and his "Dean Men's Bells" (1912) have been called Stevensonian, partly, no doubt, because they are somewhat in the vein of that exquisite romancist, and partly because, at that date, it was customary to give this name to such-like tales if they were written with any feeling for style and the magic of words.

Meanwhile, there had been a novel of a very different kind, "A Wilderness of Monkeys" (1911), a satirical study in the artistic temperament, with modern Scotland for its time and place; and, in 1911, a book of short stories, provocatively named "Above Your Heads", and said, in a preface, to have been all rejected by magazine editors as "above the heads of their readers". The stories are of varying merit, some admirable, some not remark- able, and there is a suggestion in that title that Niven was just then taking himself a little too seriously. If so, it was a passing mood, and he has long since left it behind him. With "The Porcelain Lady" (1913) he is back from the romance of the past conjuring with his then recent memories in a wholly delightful narrative of journalistic life in London, with the loves of Ruth Winter and John Brough to bring an idyllic charm into the realities of newspaper office routine. Then came the first of Niven's more uncompromisingly realistic novels, "Ellen Adair", with its vivid pictures of Edinburgh life and the inherent, unsentimentalised pathos of the unclassed Ellen. The Adair family, in all the detail of their everyday living, are drawn sympathetically and revealingly, the father, the mother, the brother, the two sisters—you are made so intimately familiar with these people that the tragedy of Ellen's downfall is the more poignant because it moves you with pity for them all—even for the genial, practical, worldly-wise Mrs. Adair whose foolish ambitions for her girls are largely the cause of the catastrophe. Here, and in "Justice of the Peace" (1914) Niven reaches his highest level of achievement. There is a sense of artifice, of carefully planned melodramatic effect in the deaths of father and son in the final chapter, otherwise "Justice of the Peace" has the unexaggerated realism, the plain truthfulness to life and character that is Niven's highest and most individual gift. Its scenes are in Glasgow, and its theme is the conflict between the strictly business ideals of the kindly, commonplace Ebenezer Moir and the artistic ideals of Martin, one of his two sons—or rather between the widely differing temperaments of Martin and his mother, for the father got over his disappointment and could sympathise with Martin and take pride in his successes, but the implacability of the mother brought about the estrangement which was only ending when Martin died in the hour of his triumph.

Niven has never gone the way to be popular. If he had worked with his eye on the public he would have concentrated on one particular kind of novel instead of following his inclination and writing whatever story came to him next. I daresay many readers of "Ellen Adair" in 1913 and "Justice of the Peace", in 1914, were rather daunted when, in 1915, they bought "Hands Up!" and found he had turned his back on the homely realism of Scottish life and was off to the Wild West in a picturesque, picaresque story of the backwoods— a capital story in its kind, with literary qualities not common to that kind of story; but not the thing to please those who prefer the uncoloured, familiar *milieu* of its two predecessors, for few readers are so catholic of taste that they can be equally interested in every variety of fiction. Niven has suffered through not accommodating himself to this human

weakness. He immediately followed "Hands Up!"
with "Two Generations" (1916), a study in heredity,
more or less in the vein of "Justice of the Peace"
and "Ellen Adair", and nearly on the same high
level with them.

So far, the critics on the whole, had crowned
him handsomely, but probably for the reasons I
have suggested, the public had been inconstant, he
had alternately attracted and repelled them by his
changes from romance to hard realism and then
back again, till many began to hold aloof, not knowing where to have him, or what he would be giving
them next. Whether it was some feeling of disappointment at this lack of the full appreciation
that was due to him or nothing but a revival of
the old wanderlust that moved him, I do not know,
but it was somewhere about this period that Niven
folded up his tent like the traditional Arab and
stole away to British Columbia. There he has
remained ever since, and has written several books
I have not seen, for I believe they were published
in America and Canada only, and he has not troubled
to find a publisher for them in this country. He
writes articles and stories for American periodicals;
I hear news of him from wandering authors who
look in at his remote home on the shores of Kootenay
Lake; now and then I get a letter from him, full
of cheerfulness and hints of the happiness he and

his wife find in their "lodge in the vast wilderness"
amid suns and snows and woods and mountains,
and all the beauty of a country whose spell has been
upon him ever since he roughed it there when he
was young. In 1923 a special edition of his "Justice
of the Peace" was issued in America, with introductions by Hugh Walpole and Christopher Morley,
and there are many of us who would say with
Walpole, "his proper place has not yet been accorded
to him either in America or England". Some day
a Prime Minister, or somebody more important than
a literary critic, will utter a word in praise of Niven
during an after-dinner speech, and all the world
will rush to read him, and there will be new editions
of his books, and he will be famous, and money
will rain down on him like manna from the skies—
if he is still alive. Meanwhile, he goes his quiet
way, far from the madding crowd, in his "shingled
house that stands among tall trees", at Nelson, B.C.,
and it seems likely that London may see him no
more. Among other books, since he went into
exile, he has published two volumes of his poems,
"Maple-Leaf Songs" (1917) and "A Lover of the
Land" (1925), and, in the latter, some verses "To
Those Who Call Me Back" make it clear that
London, "the tricky jade", London and fame
"meant never much to me", and that he is happier where he is—that, as he has it in another

poem, written at "Willow Point, Kootenay Lake,
1924":

> "From humming-birds to sleigh-bells
> I love the way life goes
> In this lost land, from one view,
> But Paradise for those
> Who love the world God gave men,
> Its Summers and its Snows."

EDWIN PUGH.

EDWIN PUGH

IT was long ago, late in the 1890's, when I first met Edwin Pugh. Even then I did not really meet him—I only saw him, and I don't think he saw me. He had published his first four books, " A Street in Suburbia ", " A Man of Straw ", " King Circumstance ", and " Tony Drum ", and was one of the guests of honour at a dinner of the New Vagabonds' Club, then at the height of its pupularity under the joint secretaryship of G. B. Burgin and Douglas Sladen. I seem to remember that Zangwill, Coulson Kernahan, and Jerome were there, and that Richard Whiteing was another of the guests of honour; but I was more particularly interested in Pugh, because he was new and strange, was just then being acclaimed in long reviews as a young novelist of brilliant promise, and because, moreover, he was writing stories of low life and I was at that date doing something in the same line myself.

Before the dinner was finished, chance brought him round near the table where I sat, and while he stood chatting with a couple of celebrities to whom Burgin had been introducing him, I noticed that he looked surprisingly young (he was, in fact, only twenty-four); that he had a short, sturdy, well set up figure, a fresh complexion, a very big black moustache (which oddly enough took nothing from his youthfulness) and the largest and brightest eyes, I think, that I have ever seen in the head of any man. The eyes have lost some of their brightness now, thirty years later, and the black moustache has turned to an iron grey, and he has supplemented it with a trim, grizzled beard, so that he makes up for looking less than his years when he was young by looking older than he is now that he is middle-aged.

Pugh comes of old Welsh stock, but was born in London, in 1874, and has lived all his life in its north-western area, except for intervals when he went as far afield as Pinner, in one direction, and Balham in the other. He must have started writing almost as soon as he could hold a pen; anyhow, when he was twelve he wrote a short story that was not only published but paid for. Also, he practised a 'prentice hand by writing three or four novels which, with a stoical discretion of which few young authors are capable, he destroyed.

Something of his schooldays, his early reading, the drab, discouraging environment in which his childhood and boyhood were passed you may gather

from " The Eyes of a Child " (1917), which I
believe his *Daily Telegraph* critic was right in
ranking as Pugh's finest achievement in contem-
plative literature, " for this Odyssey of a boy's
soul, sensitive yet serene, is written with such
delicate sympathy and knowledge of human nature
that our hearts are won as if by some intimate
companionship." The humour and pathos of it
all are admirably restrained; there is no bitterness,
no self-pity, but an abounding sympathy for less
fortunate children with whom the writer came in
contact, and a deep sense of the wrong done to
them by shutting them off from the opportunities
and happy influences that if we were really civilized
would be the common inheritance of childhood
everywhere.

I do not say that " The Eyes of a Child " is
strictly autobiographical; Pugh may have allowed
his imagination to colour and amplify some of his
experiences, as the historical novelist allows himself
to shape the facts of history to his purpose and
still keeps the whole thing true in all essentials;
I do not know; but there is certainly a good deal
of literal autobiography in it, as there is in its sequel
" The Secret Years " (1923), which takes up the
story of Tobias Morgan, who is about thirteen at
the end of " The Eyes of a Child ", and carries it
on through another eight years.

THE GLORY THAT WAS GRUB STREET

At the age of thirteen, Pugh started to earn his own living as an assistant in an iron factory, and after working three months for fourteen hours a day broke down in health and had to give it up and look for other employment. Tobias Morgan tells you in " The Secret Years " that after he left school he found employment as an errand-boy " at a little haberdashery in the Millfield Road ", but the humiliations and hardships there were more than he could endure for long, and one Saturday evening he went home and would not go back. " Three days afterwards," he says, " I saw a card on Wrenchams' factory gate in the Euston Road announcing that a Strong Boy was Wanted Within, entered the yard, was asked a few questions by the foreman, and was at once taken on. And there, for a few beatific months, at least, I was—in so far as it was in me to be—quite happy." Yet, as Tobias Morgan goes on to relate, he had to be at the factory by six in the morning, and his work there " left me little time to live:

"I seldom arrived home before nine o'clock, and then was too tired for anything but bed. Indeed, I often dozed over my supper, and fell fast asleep before I had done undressing myself—to awake in discomfort an hour or so afterwards and divest myself of the last of my clothes. On Saturdays I arrived home between four and five, and thus had the evening to myself; but there was always so much to do in the way of deferred tasks that I had no leisure for relaxation. . . . I was growing amazingly fast. My body was compact of muscle, sinew and hard bone. I was strong as a young bull. Well, a good deal of my strength I owed to my hard work and the hard knocks I had taken and given at Wrenchams'. My debt to Wrenchams' and all that Wrenchams' stood for was immeasurable. Wrenchams' was instilling in me the lore of life, its heights, its depths, its infinite complexities. Wrenchams' had taught me to laugh. It had once or twice made me cry. It had helped me to focus my outlook to right perspectives, right proportions. I knew now the bigness and the littleness of men. . . ."

The full significance of this passage comes home to you as you read the vivid character sketches of certain of the motley crew of men and boys who worked at Wrenchams', and the narration of Tobias's experiences among them, and you may take it that Pugh drew on his personal recollections for these things as Dickens drew on his for those pictures of young David Copperfield's slavery in the blacking factory.

From this arduous toil, when a few months of it had rather broken him down, tough as he had grown under the hammerings of circumstance, Pugh withdrew and, on the recommendation of a friend, secured a post in a lawyer's office, and here again you find Tobias, of " The Secret Years ", following in the footsteps of his creator. After leaving Wrenchams' he gets a new start with a firm of lawyers who have offices in King Street, Cheapside, and here, to increase his knowledge of the

world and of human nature, he is brought into touch
with types of character and phases of life that were
theretofore unknown to him. He found, he says,
that man's inhumanity to man was never more
constantly or blatantly in evidence than in a lawyer's
office:

"Against the spirit of goodwill which animates the poor,
and is to their eternal credit, must be debited that other
spirit of self-interest and ill-will which likewise plays its
part in what we are pleased to call our civilisation. Those
who have the least to spare are always the most generous;
those who have the most to waste are always the most
niggardly and grasping. It was my salvation that, both
in the manner of my descent and ascent into and out of
the ultimate deeps there were qualifying stages. Before I
entered upon that spell of drudging servitude at Wrenchams'
I had already been made free of the meaning of poverty.
And now, before I entered into possession of my manhood,
I was again to pass through the ordeal of another kind of
purgatory. I was to rid myself, this time, of any illusions
my near acquaintance with the sweet humanity of the poor
had bred in me. I was to study at first hand some very
different phases of the human comedy. I was to discover
that all men and women were not inevitably kind or even
just, as they may have seemed in the days before my first
ideals were shattered, that cupidity and spite and envy
are factors in the battle for existence almost as strong, and
often more successful, than any of the virtues. I was to
encounter falsehood and cruelty, lust and greed, in their
ugliest forms; to watch the working of little minds reaching
out slimy tentacles to grasp at paltry prizes of power and
wealth, of base motives insinuating themselves tortuously,
like the serpent in Eden, into every fair and goodly aspect
of life."

264

EDWIN PUGH

These two autobiographical novels explain what Pugh meant when he once said that London had been his best school; in its places of business and amusement; in its swarming streets; and in his dealings with all sorts and conditions of its people he learned to read the hearts of men and women and acquired the understanding of them, of their ways of thought and action, and matured the broad philosophy of life that he has put into his books. During his eight years in a city office he was spending his evenings and many of his nights in study and in writing. He began to contribute short stories to the papers, and ran a series of tales in the *Sun*, which was then flourishing under the editorship of T. P. O'Connor.

Tobias, in " The Secret Year ", opens his last chapter with the statement that " It was my twenty-first birthday. I sat alone in my lonely room. But it was not so lonely to-night. I was seeing visions, dreaming dreams. My solitude was peopled with happy ghosts, smiling faces, friendly voices. I had published a book. My first-born was alive and kicking ". And it was when he was twenty-one that Pugh published his first book, " A Street in Suburbia ". He had happened to meet Madame Sarah Grand, then in the full fame that came to her as the author of " The Heavenly Twins ", and she was so keenly interested in his work that she introduced him to her publisher, William Heinemann, and he published Pugh's first half dozen books. The four I have named at the outset were followed between 1900 and 1904 by " Mother-Sister ", " The Heritage ", " The Stumbling Block ", and " Fruit of the Vine ". All these were stories of the pathos and humour, the tragedy and everyday comedy of middle-class and lower London; and their characters, from the deplorable John Coldershaw and his mother, in " A Man of Straw ", to the wistful, fanciful " Tony Drum ", and the passionate, proud, painfully self-conscious Bria and her honest but rather simple lover, Gascon Basterfield, in " The Stumbling Block ", are not only shrewdly observed but drawn with the insight and sympathetic imagination that differentiate the realistic artist from the merely careful photographer who gets no beauty into his portrait but such as the eye can see.

This succession of books lifted Pugh into the front rank of that group of writers—Arthur Morrison, Pett Ridge, Hubert Crackanthorpe, Zangwill, and others—who were then rising to eminence as realistic interpreters of life among the London poor. But the success of his first book moved him to give up the city office and devote himself entirely to literature, and, since his work was not of a kind to make him a best-seller, and man cannot live on

praise alone, he found it necessary, after a while,
to turn his hand to more profitable pot-boiling. He
wrote a vast number of lively sketches of London
life for the *Morning Leader* and other papers, and
serials of a popular sort for divers periodicals. Of
these were " The Purple Head ", " The Spoilers ",
" The Enchantress ", " The Broken Honeymoon ".
He wrote, in 1908, an admirable study of " Charles
Dickens: The Apostle of the People "; and in 1912
one of the best of the many books that have been
written about London and the multifarious aspects
of its common life, " The City of the World ";
and, in the same year, an exhaustive account of
" The Dickens Originals ". Then he got back to
his true *genre* with " Harry the Cockney " and
" Punch and Judy " in 1913; with " The Quick
and the Dead " (1914) and in 1916 with " Slings
and Arrows ". This was succeeded by " The Eyes
of a Child ", which first appeared in the *Daily Mail*
and is I think the high-water mark of his achievement so far; and by its sequel, " The Secret Years ".
I have made free with the autobiographical elements
in these last two, but there is much autobiography
and personal experience in nearly all of them—in
" Tony Drum ", in " Harry the Cockney ", in
" Slings and Arrows ", and in his latest, " The
World is My Oyster " (1924) and " Empty Vessels "
(1926), with its satirical caricatures of literary men

and bitter pictures of literary society in the London of to-day.

That bitterness arises from nothing but an innate detestation of the shams, pretences, affectations which adulterate such society everywhere; for whatever else the years may have done to him they have left him still too much of a humorist and man of sentiment to be able to assume the part of a Timon. I remember an article in which Thomas Burke speaks of Pugh's helpful kindness to him when he was an unknown beginner and Pugh a man with a considerable reputation, and there is a revealing glimpse of Pugh's personality in that article which I will quote, both because I know it is sensitively accurate and because I could not express it so well myself. " You need not be an hour in his company," wrote Burke, " to perceive that he is a man who has been hurt and has cultivated a hide. His quiet fun and his ready chuckle tell you that; the comfortable have little to chuckle about, and the comic cannot live where suffering has not been. He is one of the many who were born in exile, and see a long way off the country where they would be. These are always lonely and always shy; and though they may learn to talk they give out little of their inwardness." But Pugh has been less reticent in his books; he has unpacked his heart in them.

268

W. PETT RIDGE

WHEN people say, as they very often do, that the
born Londoner knows little and cares less about
the city of his birth, and that it is the men born
elsewhere and becoming Londoners by adoption who
get to love and understand London most intimately,
I generally deny this, being myself a Cockney and
loyal to my tribe. But I am never anxious to argue
the point, because if the statement is not true, it
is half true, and when you come to the end of the
argument you are only back at the beginning of
it. For if you count up the authors who have most
fully and faithfully depicted the life of London
you find that too many of them are not her own
children but foundlings, as it were, to whom she has
given a home. Dickens was born at Portsea, in
Hampshire, Thackeray in India, Gissing at Wakefield, in Yorkshire. If you go farther back, though
Stow, London's ancient chronicler, and Dekker,
Ben Jonson, Defoe, who all loved the town and
pictured it vividly, were born in London, of others
who painted it as knowingly, Congreve was born
in Yorkshire, Gay near Barnstaple, Addison in

Wiltshire, Steele in Dublin, Dr. Johnson at Lich-
field, Fielding in Somersetshire. And if you come
to our own day, though I believe Arthur Morrison
(whose grimly realistic stories of London low life
have not been surpassed by any living writer) was
born in London, and know that Thomas Burke,
Frank Swinnerton and Edwin Pugh were, Neil
Lyons (and how wonderfully he translates the life
and soul of the Cockney in the humour and pathos
of his tales!) was born in South Africa; I don't
know where H. V. Morton was born: he ought to
be a native Londoner, to write as he does, but
probably is not; and Pett Ridge was born in Kent,
and he, too, has so found his way to the heart of
the town, and the town has so found its way to his
that he has grown to know and love the London
of our day as Dickens knew and loved Victorian
London.

In the nineties, the dazzling nineties when Oscar
Wilde and Aubrey Beardsley were coruscating, Pett
Ridge had arrived in London and was a clerk in the
Continental Goods Office of a great Railway Company, while his friend that was to be, the future
author of "Many Cargoes", was still keeping
accounts, a mile or two away from him, in the Post
Office Savings Bank. He had not yet emerged as
an author, but you may take it that he was consciously or unconsciously gathering material, laying

in supplies, as it were, to carry him on that new adventure.

It is a mistake to think you can form a close and reliable acquaintance with the ways of men and women by throwing over all your domestic responsibilities, segregating yourself from the crowd, in the days of your youth, and starving in a garret or luxuriating and brooding in a study; in such circumstances you can only write novels that have no real knowledge behind them of the life and character with which they deal. Dickens raged, in his later years, against the slavery and humiliations he had to endure when he worked, as a child, in a blacking factory; but that and his experiences as a reporter, in a lawyer's office, as a man who had gone about much among his fellows and shared the common joys and sorrows of everyday humanity, proved of incalculable value to him as a novelist. Gissing bitterly resented the poverty and hardship that fell to his lot, but all except the poorest of his novels have their roots in those hardships and in that poverty.

So I do not suppose Pett Ridge regrets the years he spent in the railway goods office, and nobody else will, for they must have served to give him an early introduction to that middle-class and lower London life which he has pictured with such sympathetic mastery in all its motley variations of character and event. Anyhow, he continued his office work while he was presently trying a 'prentice hand, in his leisure, at writing fiction, and before long was contributing sketches and stories, in his own name and under the pseudonym of Warwick Simpson, to divers periodicals. He had published a first book of these, "Eighteen of Them", and two or three other books, and was, he says in his sort-of-autobiography, "A Story Teller", which made its appearance in 1925, earning by the pen three times as much as he drew in salary from the goods office, before he resolved to run off the railway line and make literature his profession.

"I belonged to the period," he writes, "when the idea of a youth labelling himself 'author' and taking residence in Bloomsbury before he managed to get work into print had been given up. The royal road to literature, it was understood, now led from the Civil Service or from a business desk, and only those endowed—or impeded—with an independent income dared to take up the profession without careful and most apprehensive experiments. . . . In a general way, a novelist has to earn a living without assistance, and it is no reproach to him that he should, ere setting out on the great voyage, make a few trials on short journeys. Arnold Bennett tells me he has always practised a habit of burning his boats behind him. To do this you need, I think, first of all to see that the boats are covered by insurance; second, to make certain you have a large shipbuilding yard in working order. To the young writers who ask me for advice in procedure I always recommend caution; I can truthfully say I have ever practised it."

W. PETT RIDGE

This may seem a tame and timorous ideal, but you would realise that there is none finer or more courageous if you knew, as I do, how frequently those glorious creatures who take the more reckless path plunge their wives and children into privations, or are not too proud to levy toll, in the shape of unreturned loans, on modester men who have subdued themselves to such toil and carefulness— how frequently those glorious creatures descend inefficiently, and proudly condescend to subsist, more or less at second hand, on the fruits of that very prudence they magnificently affect to despise.

I should need more space than is at my disposal if I attempted to deal even briefly with all Pett Ridge's novels and books of short stories—in a little over thirty years they have accumulated to more than thirty. Some of his short stories, and chapters of some of his novels have a rural setting; now and then they give glimpses of foreign parts; but as a rule their scenes are in central or suburban London, and their dramatis personæ belong to those circles whose members never figure in the Court Circular. Members of the aristocracy, kindly and gracious and occasionally otherwise, may get into his pages when the tale requires them, but high life plays second fiddle to lower life when Pett Ridge calls the tune.

273

THE GLORY THAT WAS GRUB STREET

I seem to remember that all critics were not kind to his first novel, "A Clever Wife", in 1895, but it made more stir than most first novels do; and three years later—after "The Second Opportunity of Mr. Staplehurst", "Secretary to Bayne, M.P.", "Three Women and Mr. Frank Cardwell"—his fifth, "Mord Em'ly", carried him triumphantly into popular success, and still remains one of the ablest and most delightful of his books. If I were driven to direct anyone to what I count as the best thing he has done, I should be divided between the whimsical, poignant, realistic romance of that charming little Cockney, "Mord Em'ly", "A Son of the State" (an admirable story of a reformatory boy), "'Erb", "A Breaker of Laws", and "Name of Garland", or "Mrs. Galer's Business". These are personal preferences and I would not dispute the choice of any who would put "The Amazing Years" and "Well-to-do Arthur" in place of any two of my selection. Many rank him highest as a writer of short stories, and I am contented to agree that there are tales in "Up Side Streets", and other of his short-story volumes (most of which I have not reckoned in totalling his books at over thirty), that are not only as acutely observed and as deft and true in workmanship as the best of his novels but as good as the best short stories that have been written in our time.

Just as you may have heard people say of someone

they have met that he or she is "a regular Dickens character", so have I heard them say of this or that person that he or she "might almost have walked out of one of Pett Ridge's stories"; and this I take as spontaneous testimony to the vivid truthfulness of his portraiture. I have met his perky, smart office-boys in the flesh, his good-hearted, self-confident, ambitious youths, his motherly old women, his genial or stolid shopkeepers, policemen, railway-porters, his shrewd business men, bent on parochial or political honours, his flippant damsels who are out for easy happiness and do not always get it, his little lodging-house Cinderellas, his pleasant, sensible girls who work for their livings in shops or offices and manage their own families, and blundering fathers or brothers of their families, and his children of all sorts, who are among the most vital and natural children of fiction. Some of the cleverest, most intimately revealing of his character studies are in his recent "London Types", illustrated by a re-markable series of portrait-studies by E. O. Hoppé—you might read this as an introduction to the kind of people who largely inhabit Pett Ridge's literary world.

Like Dickens, he is above everything a humorist, and his sense of humour and inside knowledge of his themes keep him from exaggerating the darker side of things. He is no mere looker-on but has seen below the surface, and knows that even the direst poverty has its compensations; that love and hope and laughter survive in places where an outsider perceives nothing but squalor and gloom. "The lives of the poor", he has said, "are in the lump brighter and more amusing than those of the well-to-do middle class. Their amusements are enjoyed to the full"; and you might print that as an appropriate text on most of his title pages. He is not blind to the suffering that penury and ignorance entail; to the disadvantages against which the poor have to make such headway as they can; but he is too accurate a realist to indulge in extravagances of bestiality and sordid misery for the sake of effect. These things enter into his stories in their due proportion, are dark details of them, never the whole of them. He has learned that pathos and laughter, tragedy and comedy alternate, like night and day, that there is still some soul of happiness in lives unhappy, and that otherwise no life anywhere would be liveable.

But though he has written plenty of slum stories, he is far from being only a slum novelist. The prevailing characters in his books are city clerks, men and women who keep shops or are engaged in commercial or financial concerns, the domestic servant and the capable, up-to-date business-girl. Of this last he has drawn several examples with

extraordinary lifelikeness. She appears in his "Just
Like Aunt Bertha" (1925)—one of those sensible,
shrewd, unconventional, managing women who have
figured with differences of character and under
widely different conditions, in other of his stories.
She is essentially the modern woman, and much
more real and up-to-date than the girls who, in the
novels of authors supposed to be desperately advanced,
are presented as such because they jazz at night-
clubs, drink cocktails and are easy with their morals;
for these latter are, in fact, mere reincarnations of
early Victorian girls who in their former state
frequented Vauxhall and Cremorne Gardens and
rioted at places worse than any night-clubs, such
as the old-time Eagle in the City Road. The
essentially modern spirit is in the girls and women
who are not living the conventional, old-fashioned
"gay" life, but asserting their independence as
clerks and secretaries, as competent, practical persons
running successful businesses, competing with man
in the market-place and proving his equal, sometimes his superior, showing a genius for finance,
finding their feet in the professions and in Parliament.
These are the authentic modern women; the "gay"
sort are nothing new at all; and that particular type
of authentic modern woman has been more fully,
realistically and variously portrayed by Pett Ridge
than by any of his contemporaries.

THE GLORY THAT WAS GRUB STREET

For many years Pett Ridge lived near the heart of London, and though he has now withdrawn and makes his home on its outskirts he cannot keep away from it, but comes back from Chislehurst most days to roam its familiar streets and mingle with its motley crowds as if, like Lamb, he loved to feel himself a part of so much life. He translates his sympathy into practice, and has done generous service in alleviating the needs and brightening the lives of children in poor neighbourhoods. He is a good clubman, and one of the wittiest of platform or after-dinner speakers, giving his drollest sayings a droller touch by uttering them with an unsmiling gravity of countenance. But however stolid he may be for artistic purposes, he cannot successfully disguise his natural geniality. There is a very characteristic anecdote of how he was introduced to Mark Twain after a London dinner as "the Mark Twain of England", and while Mark was expressing his concurrence in the description, Pett Ridge interrupted, with his air of imperturbable gravity, to remark that his introducer was in error: "What he meant to say was that you are the Pett Ridge of America." "Ah," said Mark Twain delightedly, taking his arm in friendly fashion, "now I know we shall get along together!"

RAFAEL SABATINI

THERE are several ways to success in literature, and several sorts of success, and as often as not the best sort lies at the end of the longest way. Authors who take short cuts to glory generally find they have gone to the wrong place and got nothing but a flash of notoriety which leaves them in the dark again almost as soon as an admiring world has caught a glimpse of them. You will hear stories of little groups of writers who league together, as mutual aid societies, to shout each other's praises in the press and win for one another the success that none of them is strong enough to achieve for himself. These stories are not untrue, and the little groups are innocently proud of themselves, and feel very superior to more popular authors who are, in a manner, self-made men and have earned all the distinction that belongs to them single-handed and by their own work. But the reputations such *coteries* manufacture for each other consist more of noise than of substance, and as soon as they grow tired of making the noise there is little or nothing left for any of them.

THE GLORY THAT WAS GRUB STREET

To say nothing of the tinsel, artificial glories of that order, it would be a sad volume that chronicled the meteoric careers of the many authors who have burst into notoriety with a lucky first book but have lost ground with every book they published after and spent years in climbing back to the level they rose from, to settle down there at last among the have-beens who will never be again and console themselves by cherishing,

> "with empty boasts and proud regrets,
> Remembrance of a name
> The world forgets."

It would be easy to compile a long list of living poets and novelists who have rioted through that immortal hour and have now subsided upon hours that are merely mortal. Far happier than these are the men who instead of beginning too early begin too late, as William De Morgan did, and in their latter days are crowned with a success they cannot live long to enjoy. But happiest of all are the authors who begin in good time and, even though they endure neglect for many seasons, go on doing good work and waiting until, without any adventitious aids, solely by virtue of what they have done and are doing, arrive at recognition and rewards which they have earned twice over; for the reputation that matures so slowly, being a natural and sturdy growth, is slow to die.

One of these latter authors is Rafael Sabatini; in a quiet way his life has been nearly as romantic as any of his books. His father was an Italian, Maestro Cav. Vincenzo Sabatini, who married an English-woman, Anna Trafford. He was born at Jesi, in Central Italy, and educated at the École Cantonate of Zuog, in Switzerland, and at the Lycée of Oporto, Portugal. I believe he was brought to England while he was still young; anyhow, for all his school-ing in Switzerland and Portugal, like Conrad, who was born and reared in Poland; like W. L. George, who was born in France and through all his earlier years could speak nothing but French; like Caradoc Evans who spoke his native Welsh and knew little or no English when he first arrived in London; Sabatini has acquired a richer vocabulary and writes an easier, more virile and vigorous English than do many distinguished authors who were born in England and expensively trained in its Public Schools and Universities. Coming to Eng-land, he made his home at Liverpool, and worked for a while on a Liverpool newspaper. He wrote short stories and, like most beginners, had manu-scripts rejected and accepted by the magazines; and during this time, and before and after this, he must have devoted himself largely to that wide

study of Italian, Spanish and French history which
was to bear such good fruit in the romances, plays,
biographies and historical works that were ultimately to yield him his due meed in money as well
as in fame—ultimately, for the due meed was in
no haste to bestow itself upon him, and he had a
lingering interval of hopes deferred and difficulties
to be overcome such as have soured and embittered
many authors, but he seems to have taken the worst
as he has taken the best of things with a philosophical
impartiality, so that success has left him what he
was in the days of his probation, one of the kind-
liest, most gracious and most modest of men. I
daresay it was his native modesty that helped to
prolong the period of his waiting. I have the
best of reasons to know that he never had any skill
in pushing himself, and that he had not even a
rudimentary knowledge of that art of self-advertisement which others use to such prompt and profitable
effect. His only method seems to have been to
do his books, and do them well, and to leave
them to do all the rest, and in the end they have
done it in the most satisfactory and triumphant
manner.

Born in 1875, he is now a year or two over fifty,
and his first novel, " The Tavern Knight ", appeared
when he was close on thirty, in 1904. In these
twenty-four years he has written over twenty books

and some three or four plays; and you realise what
this must have meant in unremitting industry if
you remember that the books included, apart from
imaginative fiction, such exacting and scholarly
histories as " The Life of Cæsar Borgia ", and
" Torquemada and the Spanish Inquisition ", though
he cannot have given much less time to reading and
research for the groundwork of his historical romances
and for the brilliant series of historical studies and
stories in his two volumes of " The Historical
Nights' Entertainment ".

His second novel, " Bardelys the Magnificent ", is
a gallant, picturesque romance of the France of
Louis XIII, written with a gusto and imaginative
power that should have carried him straightway
into a resounding popularity; if it fell short of
doing that, it at least established him alike with the
public and with the critics as a novelist who knew
how to tell an excellent story and to tell it, moreover, with more of literary art than commonly goes
to the making of popular novels. I have seen this
and other of his stories compared with the tales
of Dumas, and certainly Dumas would have gloried
in the dashing, riotously romantic Bardelys, who,
flown with wine, wagers that he will win and marry
a girl who is a stranger to him, and is too fine a
gentleman not to repent of this swaggering boast
but, having gone through desperate adventures

which cunningly hold the reader in continual expectation and suspense, ends by gaining the lady after he has lost his wager. There is a Dumas-like breeziness and gusto in the telling of all this, but there is more finish of style, and a subtler psychology in the presentation of character than were ingredients in the magic of the great French master.

Following Bardelys at yearly intervals came " The Trampling of the Lilies ", " Love at Arms ", " The Shame of Motley ", " St. Martin's Summer ", " Anthony Wilding ", " The Lion's Skin ", then, in 1912 (with the " Life of Cæsar Borgia " in the same year) " The Justice of the Duke "; in 1913 (with the history of " Torquemada " in that same year) came " The Strolling Saint ", and in the next four years " The Gates of Doom ", " The Sea Hawk ", " The Banner of the Bull ", and " The Snare ". These last three added very appreciably, I think, to Sabatini's steadily increasing vogue. In 1918 and 1919 came the two volumes of " The Historical Nights' Entertainment "; then, after an interval of two years, we had " Scaramouch ", with " Captain Blood " and " Fortune's Fool " on its heels in 1922 and 1923, and the " Sabatini boom " had begun.

It seemed to begin suddenly with " Scaramouch ", but might very well have started with any of the three preceding novels if they had not been published during the war—with " The Sea Hawk ", a glamorous, robust story of Barbary corsairs and a great sea-rover, Sir Oliver Tressilian, whose wild adventures are related with touches of grim humour and in the finest spirit of romance; with " The Banner of the Bull ", written round the dazzling, strange career of Cæsar Borgia and alive with the intrigues and clashing ambitions and rich in the scenic magnificence of mediæval Italy; with " The Snare ", a vividly dramatic romance of Portugal during the Peninsular War, which he adapted for the stage, a little later, in collaboration with Leon M. Lion, who produced it successfully at the Savoy Theatre.

Meanwhile Sabatini had already produced, with less success, three other plays, including a version, dramatised in collaboration with Henry Hamilton, of " Bardelys the Magnificent "; and had occupied himself for a while as partner in a London publishing firm. But he had done with publishing when ' Scaramouch " appeared, to take the reading world by storm and set an enthusiastic public asking for his earlier books and stir the publishers to run after him, who had hitherto been running after them.

He had fared until then no better in America than in his own country, and I have heard that no sooner was his name one to conjure with than certain American houses made various efforts to secure novels of his they had formerly declined to accept.

THE GLORY THAT WAS GRUB STREET

" Scaramouch " was filmed, and triumphed sensationally on both sides of the Atlantic; and, in a word, after twenty years in the wilderness Sabatini had emerged into a long-promised land that is flowing with milk and honey every pint and pound of which he had paid for in honest, hard work long before the good were delivered to him.

Most writers of romance avoid the risk of overstraining their imaginations by inventing a formula at the outset, and thereafter make all their books according to that pattern. One of the charms of Sabatini's work results from his never having adopted that easy-going plan. Each new romance of his has been always a new one and never the old one artfully retold with variations. It has not only the freshness of a new plot but usually of different surroundings. Bardelys flourished in seventeenth century France; " The Justice of the Duke " is another Borgian story; " The Sea Hawk " is all of the sea and piracy; " The Snare " takes you into the Napoleonic wars, and " Scaramouch " into the horrors and heroisms of the French Revolution. " Captain Blood " grows out of the Monmouth rising and the tyrannies of Bloody Jeffreys. Sabatini has a delicate skill in the creation of heroines, but the love element is only one of various threads of interest in his stories. He handles the facts of history imaginatively, and turns them to effective account when they serve his purposes; when he introduces real notabilities into his narrative he draws them with fullness of knowledge and yet with such deftness that though they are clothed in all the actuality that once belonged to them that are so nicely toned to his general scheme that they do not overshadow or take anything from the lifelikeness of his fictitious persons. His Louis XIII in " Bardelys the Magnificent " is a masterpiece of realistic portraiture; as that is of Jeffreys in "Captain Blood "; there are graphic sketches in " The Snare " of Wellington and of the famous secret service agent, Colonel Colquhoun Grant; and notable pen-pictures of Robespierre, Danton and Marat on the crowded canvas of " Scaramouch."

I remember reading an interview in which Sabatini laid it down that, whatever his *genre*, the aim of every novelist should be the achievement of realism; that however imaginative a story may be it should be so written that a reader may feel able to accept it as true. He protested against the " over-educated sterility " of the school of novelists who, making realism an end in itself, instead of a means to an end, laboriously overload their pages with minute and sometimes unsavoury details, as if the business of the artist were not to learn how to achieve an effect of reality by selecting his material and sug-gesting more than he in fact revealed, but to rest content in a slavish imitation of the mechanical work of the average photographer. If grimness and drabness and squalor are not excluded from Sabatini's romances, they are never introduced for their own sakes, but only when they happen to be an indispensable part of his story. He is a romancist in grain, and an artist in romance, and, like the true artist, mixes his colours, as Sir Joshua said they ought to be mixed, " with brains ".

The passion for romance is too deeply rooted in our nature ever to be eradicated, but it is not always potent; it has its winters. There are fashions in fiction, as in everything else, but yesterday's modes will be in favour again to-morrow. Romance was in the ascendant once more, some years ago, when Stanley Weyman, Rider Haggard, Anthony Hope, J. M. Barrie were young; we have wandered since through arid regions of psycho-analytical experiment where no romance brightened, and Sabatini's mistake was in getting born out of his due time. But it is a hopeful augury nowadays that so many have come and are coming to him, and to such as him, drawn to his and their books for change and refreshment, as travellers are attracted to a welcome oasis in a desert.

MRS. C. A. DAWSON SCOTT

IF there is a busier novelist in London than Mrs.
Dawson Scott I have not met her (or him), and
she is so busy with such a number of things that
one is left wondering how she has found time to
write the novels and poems that have not yet yielded
her all the reputation she has earned. When she
first came to London she knew nobody, and, realising
what it meant to be without friends in a large city,
as soon as her books had made her known and
given her some influence, she founded, in 1917, the
To-Morrow Club as a centre for young and lonely
writers, and a means of bringing them in touch
with writers who were neither lonely nor necessarily
young. I have pleasant recollections of going to
that Club in its early days, when it met in a large
room that was filled with stuffed fish in glass cases
and with an audience of a much livelier kind that
sat in chairs and on the floor and heckled its lec-
turers in a manner that was fearless and free. In
1921 Mrs. Dawson Scott extended her activities and,
making the world her parish, started the P.E.N.
Club, with the idea of creating international good-

289

will and, under the presidency of John Galsworthy, the Club has grown into a vast organisation with branches in great and small countries all over the habitable globe. The mere prospect of the labour involved in all this reduces me to a paralytic state of mind, but Mrs. Dawson Scott moves among these ramifications with a godlike calm, welcoming foreign authors and making them at home when they come to England, attending meetings in America, France, Belgium, Germany and other distant places—always unperturbed, genial, hospitable, always busy about the comfort and welfare of others, and at the same time writing a new novel, editing a book or two, contributing articles to newspapers or magazines, as if she had more than the usual number of hands and at least twice as many hours in her day as are allotted to the rest of us.

Although Mrs. Dawson Scott was born—as the Cornish say—"east o' Truro", she has many relatives in the Duchy, has spent much of her time there, and has a very strong interest in its people and an intimate knowledge of them, as every reader of her novels will know. H. D. Lowry, the poet, was her cousin. "My friendship with him began", she tells me, "when we were both children and I stayed in the old Bank house at Camborne. I found in him the one among my many cousins who had the same ambition—we both wanted to write poetry, and even then we were both writing it". That good friend of young writers, *Chambers's Journal* (in which Hardy, Stanley Weyman, and others who were afterwards to become famous, made their first appearance in print), accepted their poems, and, so encouraged, Mrs. Dawson Scott presently brought out two books in quick succession: "Sappho", an epic, with woman's rights for its theme, and "Idylls of Womanhood", a series of narrative poems about women.

She had started earning her living at secretarial work when she was eighteen, and after the appearance of those two books wrote no more for several years; for marriage presently brought the cares of a family upon her and she was kept busy enough with the bringing up of her children. It often happens that, after marriage, a woman sacrifices any artistic gifts she may have on the domestic altar and loses first the inclination, then the capacity for literary work. There are exceptions. When George Eliot allied herself to George Henry Lewes, and adopted his family, she never allowed herself to become absorbed in household affairs, and while she was in her study nobody, not even Lewes himself, dared to knock at the door and break in upon her inspirations. But other women—and I believe Mrs. Oliphant was one—have wonderful powers of detachment, and do not require complete seclusion

before they can concentrate on imaginative work:
the children may be playing around them in the
same room without disturbing them; a servant may
interrupt them with an urgent message or to ask
for directions, and they can at once come out of
the world in which they had been dreaming into
the world of common day, discuss such matters of
fact efficiently, and promptly pick up the pen and
the thread of the dream again and go on as if they
had never been disturbed.

I picture Mrs. Dawson Scott working in such
circumstances. Anyhow, after her youngest child
was past the nursery stage, her natural impulse
reasserted itself, and she sat down and wrote her
first novel, "The Story of Anna Beames", a realistic
story of grim truthfulness and power—the story of
an average woman of little understanding or experience who, past her first youth, succumbs to the
attractions of Stephen Barclay, a crude, human
animal, an earthy creature, soulless, pitiless, drawn
with a subtlety of skill and insight that give vigour
of life and reality to as grimly sinister a figure as
any I remember in recent fiction. The critics are
too often blamed for neglecting new writers, but
they gave full and generous recognition to the
literary quality of Mrs. Dawson Scott's first novel,
to the knowledge and strength in its characterisation,
and the sure art with which its drab tragedy was

wrought. I read it on its first appearance, and have not read it since, but I have not lost the impression it left on me and, from my memory of it, I have always ranked "Anna Beames" as one of the ablest and most powerful of all her novels.

It was followed in 1908 by "The Burden", and in quick succession by "Treasure Trove", "Madcap Jane", "The Agony Column", "Mrs. Noakes", and "The Caddis-Worm"—the name suited to Catherine Blake who, married to a successful, bullying doctor, hides her real strength of character under an assumption of meek submissiveness, until circumstances deliver the tyrannical husband whom she loves, into her hands and she resolutely secures independence and comfort for herself and her children. There are touches of comedy in this and "The Agony Column", but in general a sombre atmosphere, a sense of the ironies and tragedies of chance and circumstance broods over all these novels, except "Madcap Jane", which is the lively, humorous holiday romance of a rebellious wife who, married (like the very different Elizabeth, in "The Burden") to a husband much older than herself, runs away to be a domestic servant and disturb the peace of another household before she is reconciled to going back home to "be good".

From Cornwall, in her early years, Mrs. Dawson Scott came to London, and she attributes the awakening of that understanding and cosmopolitan friendliness she has for people of other nations to the fact that she went to school at the Anglo-German College in Camberwell. But this in no way undermined her local patriotism; as Kipling found,

> "God gave all men all earth to love,
>   But, since man's heart is small,
> Ordains for each one spot shall prove
>   Beloved over all,"

and even, later on, when she was settled down to live and work in London, as often as opportunity came she returned for a holiday interval to her own place. Shortly before the appearance of "The Caddis-Worm" (1914), the delicate health of one of her children led her to carry him off for a long stay in a remote, little known part of Cornwall, where they lived and slept out of doors, and as she is descended from Johnny Armstrong, of Gilnockie, whose mother was a gipsy, that unconventional way of life, she says, came natural to ther both. Moreover, this long sojourn among the country people of the Duchy prompted her to write a series of novels which have Cornwall for background and Cornish folk for their characters—a series that began in 1919 with "Wastralls", and included "The Headland", "The Haunting", "They Green Stones", and in 1926, "Blown by the Wind". To these

294

were added, in 1927, "Wheal Darkness", a novel of Cornish tin-mining life, which had been left unfinished by her cousin, H. D. Lowry, and was completed and largely rewritten by Mrs. Dawson Scott. In the same year as "Wastralls" (1919) came "Against the Grain", a brilliant study in the character of an independent, self-willed, amoral boy and man who, with hardly any sense of honesty or honour, fights for his own hand, and is so sympathetically revealed that though he is not admirable he remains likeable, not only to men and women of his story but to the reader of it.

Beginning, like most authors, by writing poetry, Mrs. Dawson Scott seems to have turned again to that medium while she was working on the Cornish novels and in 1923 collected her later verse in "Bitter Herbs". Here, in tune with the tendency of the day, she writes *vers libre ;* it suits her themes and she uses it effectively and without any of the eccentricities that often mar the work of other and noisier practitioners of this art. There is the same sombre atmosphere and rural setting and the same distinctive personality in her verse as in her novels, and certain of the succession of "dramatic poems" tell of such characters, and such tales of them, as are in "The Headland" and "Mrs. Noakes". In one of these poems, "Beloved Wife of——", for instance, a husband complains that his wife, who has died in hospital, sent for their children, at the last, but not for him, and asks,

> "What did I do?
> Not more'n others; still
> They extry women, they'm the deuce!
> Adam, he held to Eve, he did,
> Because the Lord had made'n, one and one;
> And yet I lay
> The man went often to his garden hedge
> An' looked . . ."

But, he urges, "the woman was nought"; she drew other men from their farms, Tom, Alick and Jack, who loved their wives none the less, and he loved his and will follow her to her grave and cut deep in the stone over her, "Beloved wife of Job Nancarrow", so that she shall see those words when she rises on the Judgment day, and they shall speak for him.

It is exactly the sort of incident that would have fitted harmoniously into one of her novels, or into the collection of her Cornish and other short stories, "The Vampire" (1925). "Kitty Leslie at the Sea" in 1927, is another Cornish story, but an irresponsible diversion, an airy trifle in the whimsical, light comedy manner of "Madcap Jane". Clever, and entertaining, and not meant to be anything more.

The best of Mrs. Dawson Scott's work is, I think, in "The Story of Anna Beames", "Mrs. Noakes", "The Burden", "Wastralls", "The Headland" and "The Haunting". There is something of the dark-

MRS. C. A. DAWSON SCOTT

ling imagination of the Brontës in these, something
of the stark realism and grim power of Hardy,
and of his relentlessness in portraying the weaknesses
of the flesh, the frailties, passions, incontinencies of
mortal women and men. But Mrs. Dawson Scott
does not so much expose the worst side of a
character as show you all sides, and the worst
happens to be there. Some of her people, superficially civilised, are almost as raw and unregenerate
in grain as if they were survivals from the Stone
Age, but she has and communicates to her reader
such a tolerant understanding of them that you no
more dislike them for their natural errors than you
admire others for the virtues and graces that are
theirs by accidents of birth and heredity.

Those two half-brothers in "The Haunting"—
Pascoe Corlyon, the wanderer, a callous betrayer
of women, genial, attractive, but so grasping in his
dealings with his brother, Gale, that Gale, to save
himself from being reduced to penury, murders him
on the night before he was to have sailed to Jamaica
and safely buries the body in the cellar under the
house—the one brother is scarcely more sordid and
degenerate than the other, yet you are moved to
have some sympathy with both, especially with
Gale when he is haunted, obsessed, driven at last
to destruction by the implacable wraith of the mur-
dered man.

THE GLORY THAT WAS GRUB STREET

For all its dealings with the occult, its spectre, its belief in love charms and the evil eye, "The Haunting" keeps throughout a convincing air of reality; possibly because such superstition, a belief in such things, does still persist in remote parts of Cornwall; possibly because Mrs. Dawson Scott is writing here of things that are so real, so matter-of-fact to her that her very sincerity in writing of them makes them seem as real to her reader, at least for a reading while. She is an occultist possessed of psychic faculties which may perhaps be traceable to that gipsy strain in her ancestry, and you will know how sincere she is in this faith if you have read the record of her psychic experiences in "Four From the Dead".

One is left wondering why, having the keen sense of humour to which "Madcap Jane" and "Kitty Leslie" bear witness, she uses little or no humour in her finer and more serious novels? I suspect it is their prevailing sombreness that has prevented those novels from making a wider appeal than they do. Why she so segregates her humour in some books, and her greater gifts of realistic narration and characterisation in others, is more than I can say; but one day, I feel sure, she will blend these qualities of laughter and gloom, of genial comedy and tragedy in one book, as inextricably as they are blended in life itself, and that will be a popular book as well as a good one.

298

TRESIDDER SHEPPARD

ALFRED
TRESIDDER SHEPPARD

If a young man, ambitious of a professional career, wishes to become a lawyer, physician, clergyman, officer in the Army or Navy, he has to go through a settled course of study, pass examinations, and obtain certificates, but if his ambitions run in the direction of literature, he is not required to attend classes, to be harried by an examiner and get himself duly certified before he can set up in that profession: he may start practising without anybody's permission whenever he chooses; or, rather, whenever he finds that he can. The world at large is his university, and all its men and women are his teachers, usually as involuntarily as he is their pupil. He may come to literature through a blacking factory, a lawyer's office and a newspaper office, as Dickens did; through a draper's shop, like Wells; through the Post Office, like Trollope and W. W. Jacobs; through medicine, like Somerset Maugham, Warwick Deeping and Conan Doyle; through the church like Ernest Raymond and George Birmingham; through the law like Galsworthy and Philip Guedalla; and often you will find in his books traces of his early experience in those businesses or professions, and often you will not.

There must be something romantic and inspiring in the atmosphere to be breathed within the precincts of Insurance Companies, for their offices have fostered the gifts of at least four present-day men of letters, yet without leaving any noticeable marks on the literary work they have done. If any influences of the Insurance office are perpetuated in the poetry of John Drinkwater and John Freeman, or in the novels of Eden Phillpotts and Alfred Tresidder Sheppard they are either so subtle that I have missed them, or so slight that I have forgotten them. There is no rule in these matters. The East India House gets into Lamb's essays, and his stained-glass works into De Morgan's novels; but there is no smack of the surgery in Keats's poetry, and none of his life as a Controller of the Customs in Chaucer's.

So, to say nothing just now of the other three, though Tresidder Sheppard spent fifteen years in an Insurance office that was never his spiritual home. He is on both sides of his family of Devon and Cornish ancestry, but not until he came to write "Brave Earth", his seventh novel, did he lay the scenes of a story in his own West Country. He was educated at Bishop's Stortford, in Essex, and while he was keeping books for that London Insurance Company wrote, in his leisure, a first book of his

ALFRED TRESIDDER SHEPPARD

own, "The Red Cravat" (1905)—a romance which carried him far enough away from the business of the office into the past and out to the Prussia of the rough-minded and rough-handed King Frederick William, father of Frederick the Great. The buffooneries, intriguings, coarse humours and brutal tyrannies of the Prussian Court, the King and his motley entourage are presented skilfully, and with a knowledge of and insight into the life and character of the period which are as the first sprightly runnings of that feeling for the romance of history and the power to realise and re-create it which have reached such potent maturity in Sheppard's later books. The adventures of the wandering young Englishman Dick Catherwood, in "The Red Cravat", and the dangers and disasters into which he is carried by his love for the charming Joan Crystal, may be imaginary, but the intolerably harsh Prussian military system which was founded by Frederick William and in which Catherwood becomes involved, the whole setting of the story and many of its people are rescued from historical archives and made real and vividly alive again in a tale which amply fulfils the promise of the poem that preludes it:

> "Out of their dusty box, the Past,
> Where Time has shut them up so fast,
> I take these creatures of a day
> To make them puppets for my play

THE GLORY THAT WAS GRUB STREET

Old men-at-arms, whose bugles wake
No echoes now in pine and brake;
Dim ladies who, with dainty feet,
Shall trip no more in court or street;

Jesters and courtiers, in the dust,
Lying where fifes and firelocks rust,
And fans and swords and tarnished lace,
With their dead owners find a place.

Old summer days and winter fires
I bring again . . ."

That same prelude might have served for Tresidder Sheppard's next novel, "Running Horse Inn", though here he is only back at the beginning of the nineteenth century, instead of farther off at the beginning of the eighteenth. For this is a story of the years after Waterloo when George Kenneth, reported as killed, returns home on the day the girl he had loved has married his brother John. From this dramatic opening the romance develops slowly into tragedy. Though there are strong ties of affection between the brothers, after a while, with all his resolve to make the best of things, George finds that to live at the old inn under the same roof with the girl who should have been his wife, and is his brother's, is more than he can bear, but even its tragic climax, in a day when happy endings were all the fashion, could not prevent a book so brilliantly written and so intensely and naturally human in

its story from being sensationally successful..
"Running Horse Inn" was also produced, I believe,
while Tresidder Sheppard was still toiling "at the
desk's dead wood" in the Insurance office. He
sent it to that admirable but short-lived daily, the
Tribune, which was then just advertised as getting
ready to start, and it was promptly accepted by
Philip Gibbs, the *Tribune's* literary editor, and made
its appearance as the first serial to be run in that
paper. It helped to give the *Tribune* the general
reputation for excellence it maintained through its
too-brief existence, and I remember when it was
re-issued as a book in 1907 how it swept at once
into popularity.

But having achieved this notable success Tresidder
Sheppard fell almost silent; a breakdown in health
for some years interrupted the progress of his career.
When he resumed work it was to turn from historical
fiction to that bizarre, realistic, darkly imaginative
odyssey of the modern world, "The Rise of Ledgar
Dunstan" (1916), and its equally impressive,
strangely moving sequel, "The Quest of Ledgar
Dunstan" (1917). These were written as one book,
but cut in two because of their great length, and
should some day, before long, be reissued in a
single volume. "A Son of the Manse" is the one
novel of Sheppard's I have not read, but even if it
confirms the Ledgar Dunstan novels in showing

that he has a Dostoievsky-like tempestuous energy of thought and a starkly realistic narrative skill for handling problems of contemporary life and character, you still feel, looking at what he had done before and has done since, that his native bent is toward the romance of other days, and in such romance his imaginative and creative gifts reach their fullest and highest expression.

In "The Autobiography of Judas Iscariot" (1920) he has escaped again from the big but ephemeral realities of the twentieth century to the eternal realities of twenty centuries ago, and the coming of that Gospel of Love which nowadays consoles the poor and has furnished the rest of us, who still find it impracticable, with a respectable and not unprofitable profession. The theme is handled reverently and with distinction; there is no attempt to be unconventional in presenting the gracious figure of Christ; in reconstructing the character of Judas and tracing his career from boyhood to the time of the great betrayal there is no indulgence in fantastic subtleties of psychology in order to white-wash and endow him with fine motives that may ennoble or excuse his actions. Here, as in his secular romances, Sheppard gives his imagination free play in deducing details of circumstance, incident, description, dialogue from what is known, and his historic sense prevents him from inventing startling theories and treating them as facts, and holds him to a revivifying but faithful interpretation of such actual records as have come down to us.

Perhaps this very conscientiousness hampered him here; anyhow, "The Autobiography of Judas Iscariot", interesting and able though it is, remains a minor achievement and not to be ranked with those novels in which the story and its chief characters are his own, and he has only gone to literal history for atmosphere, colour, environment, for incidents and famous personages that belong to its period and can be so adapted and made part of the narrative as to give the whole an air of verisimilitude. Into his next novel, "Brave Earth", for instance, he introduces certain famous personages and historic events of the sixteenth century—in France Humphry Arundell has talk with Rabelais; in the later stages of the romance Humphry heads the religious revolt against the New Prayer Book —but the story is the story of Humphry Arundell, his early life in Cornwall, his training in France for a military career, his return home to plunge into gallant adventures in which the delightful, provocative Jackett Coffin has her share, and, after much of "feasts and merrymakes and wars," to pay the penalty for leading that desperate rebellion and lay down his life at Tyburn.

THE GLORY THAT WAS GRUB STREET

The tone and spirit, social and political, of sixteenth century England is not more cunningly recaptured in "Brave Earth" than is the earlier England of the days of the Crusades, of Kings Richard I and John and the signing of Magna Charta, by the novel that three years later, in 1927, succeeded this. It has been said, and there was no exaggeration in the saying, that we have had no greater historical romance than Tresidder Sheppard's "Here Comes an Old Sailor" since Reade wrote "The Cloister and the Hearth". In its freedom from eccentricities of style, in its mellow humour, grace of language and sensitive feeling for the things that touch common lives with beauty I think it even surpasses Reade's masterpiece. You have a hint in his foreword of how long and deeply he delved into all manner of popular and obscure chronicles of the Middle Ages before he sat down to weave this strange, delectable tale of those far-off times when magic and witchcraft were articles of common faith, when the most grotesque legends and superstitions were accepted as ordinary matters of fact, when a robust common-sense was not proof against the workings of enchantment and the evil eye, and miracles still happened because few were so incredulous as to doubt them. "Here in a frame of history," says the author, in his preliminary note, "is a legend, or piecing together of legends, half as old as man. And much of the history is of itself perforce legendary, though I have kept as nearly to facts as my authorities will permit."

The story is related by a man who is believed to have returned from the dead; Death and the Devil, in visible shapes, are among the *dramatis personæ;* and you are subtly prepared to acquiesce in these and other supernatural manifestations by the leisurely opening episodes which picture the lives of the monks in their monastery at Reculver and tell how the idealistic young Virgilius found the drowned sailor washed up one stormy night by the sea, and saw him marvellously brought back from the other world as he lay in the glimmering candle-light before the altar, waiting for burial.

Those monks of Reculver, from the grave, wise, kindly Dean Gisbert, the various brethren, old, middle-aged, simple, superstitious, homely, quaint, genial, gloomy or salacious, to the gentle visionary Virgilius, are sketched and made real with an uncompromising insight, and this intimate acquaintance with them prepares your mind for the sequel, subdues you to a mood in which you can not only surrender yourself to the interest of the story but can enjoy it and take for granted its supernatural as well as its natural developments, for a reading-while, as readily and understandingly as they would have been taken by mediæval readers.

THE GLORY THAT WAS GRUB STREET

It is Virgilius who, prompted by his brother monks, tries very cautiously to induce the drowned sailor to reveal what he can recollect of that other world from which he is so miraculously returned. But the man is reticent, or cannot remember, and, under advice, Virgilius persuades him to go back to the beginning and tell of himself, of people he had known and the adventures he had come through when he was living near by at Fordwich and Canterbury and fighting in foreign parts. He hoped in this way to lead him on through the record of his career till when he came to the manner of his death he would spontaneously continue and disclose what happened to him after, until his eyes opened again on the earth he had left. And this tale, when he has written it all out in his own fashion, Virgilius reads aloud evening after evening to the inmates of the monastery, and the comments of the gracious old Dean and the monks, between the chapters, add piquancy and something of suggestion to an alluring, curiously original narrative that is at once good history in essence, good romance and good literature.

Still, I should guess, not more than about fifty, Tresidder Sheppard is to be seen occasionally in London, and sometimes to be heard there, for of late he has been lured on to platforms and proved himself an admirable lecturer. But he gives only his leisure to London; his home and workplace is in the quiet little old-world Essex town of Saffron Walden, where he is nowadays deep in a new romance which has for its leading person one who makes a wistful, rather despised, unsuccessful figure on the stage of English history, but—since I gather that patient researches have brought to light enough to show he has been much misunderstood and mis-judged—will make a pathetically baffled, dignified, sagacious, even modestly heroic figure when he emerges, moulded to his just proportions, from the sympathetic hand that gave us "Running Horse Inn", "Brave Earth" and "Here Comes an Old Sailor".

H. M. TOMLINSON.

H. M. TOMLINSON

IF journalism could do as much for all men of
letters as it may seem to have done for H. M. Tomlinson, it might almost be accepted as a general
law that the best way of learning the literary art
is to serve an apprenticeship in a newspaper office.
But it would not be safe to give all that credit to
journalism and regard him as a precedent. He
served that apprenticeship; for over twenty years
he has been among the masters of the journalistic
craft; but his mind, unlike the dyer's hand, has
never been subdued to what it worked in. It would
be truer, I think, to say that journalism gave him
nothing but a larger knowledge of life; it did not
teach him how to write—he took that gift with
him when he went to it, and he has so much of
individuality and strength of character that it was
not able to take it away from him, as it is said to
have taken it away from so many who have been
easily subservient to its influences. When he
gathered his journalism into books it was recognised
as literature. It smells neither of the typewriter
nor of the lamp; you would guess that his feeling

for the beauty of words is as natural, as unselfconscious, as sincere as are his sensitive human sympathies and his intense feeling for the varying beauty—homely, gracious, sinister—of city and jungle, sea and mountain, day and darkness, storm and halcyon weather. To call him a stylist might suggest that with a lapidary cunning he cultivates a style. His style may be cultivated but it is without apparent artifice; his imagination does not so much play with jewelled phrases and the splendid word as it plays over a whole sentence and, using a familiar, conversational manner, clothes his thought simply or finely in language that is in keeping with it, and wonderfully effective without ever seeming to strain after any effect.

Tomlinson was born down Poplar way in 1873, and in " London River " he gives this vivid sketch of the home of his childhood there, with its significant reference, in the opening lines, to the early death of his father:

"I well remember a room from which such survivals were saved when the household ship ran on a coffin, and foundered. It was a front parlour in one of the streets with an Oriental name; which I cannot be expected to remember, for when I was last in that room I was lifted to sit on one of its horsehair chairs, its seat like a hedgehog, and I was cautioned to sit still. It was rather a long drop to the floor from a chair for me in those days. . . . That was a room for holy days, too, a place for good behaviour, and boots profaned it. . . . The room was always sombre. Light filtered into it through curtains of wire gauze, fixed in the window by mahogany frames. Over the door by which you entered was the picture of an uncle, too young and jolly for that serious position, I thought then, with his careless neckcloth, and his cap pulled down over one eye. The gilt moulding was gone from a corner of the picture—the only flaw in the prim apartment—for once that portrait fell to the floor, and on the very day, it was guessed, that his ship must have foundered. A round table set on a central thick leg having a three-clawed foot was in that chamber, covered with a cloth on which was worked a picture from the story of Ruth. But only puzzling bits of the latter were to be seen, for on the circumference of the table-cover were books, placed at precise intervals apart, and in the centre was a huge Bible with a brass clasp. With many others, my name was in the Bible, and my birthday, and a space left blank for the day of my death. . . .

"I remember a black sofa, which smelt of dust, an antimacassar over its head. That sofa would wake to squeak tales if I stood on it to inspect the model of a ship in yellow ivory resting on a wall-bracket above. There were many old shells in the polished brass fender, some with thick orange lips and spotted backs; others were spirals of mother-o'-pearl, which took different colours for every way you held them. You could get the only sound in the room by putting the shells to your ear. Like the people of the portraits, it was impossible to believe the shells had ever lived. The inside of the grate was filled with white paper, and the trickles of fine black dust which rested in its crevices would start and run stealthily when people walked in the next room. . . ."

You figure him, a small boy, a singularly observant small boy, wandering through the crowded Poplar streets, growing familiar with the bizarre appearance

313

of Lascar and Chinese, with all the motley elements
of the British and foreign seafaring community that
swarms in those parts; wandering through the
streets or loitering about the docks watching the
big ships coming in from or setting out on long
voyages and, with the roving tradition in his blood
and reminders of it in the sights and sounds that
were all around him, probably dreaming of a time
when, on some such ship as he saw emptying its
cargo at his feet, or shouldering off down the Thames
on its way to the open sea, he, too, would go adventuring into far countries which, until now, he had
only read of in books.

I know nothing of his schooling; but should guess
that he had not gone through the usual Public School
and University training, because he has such a
much wider understanding of humanity in general
and a surer, finer instinct for the potentialities of
his native language than are commonly possessed
by authors who have obtained their knowledge in
those orthodox ways. As soon as he was old
enough to start earning a livelihood, he became a
junior clerk in a shipping office in Leadenhall Street,
and here again he was kept in touch with the business and romance of those who go down to the
sea in ships, and was presently giving his evenings
to writing, and getting articles accepted by divers
periodicals. But it was a good many years before

he could emancipate himself from that office drudgery and escape on the first of the voyages that have
yielded him material for at least six of his books.

Editors were not slow to appreciate the distinctive qualities of his writing, and I take it that nothing
but the innate diffidence which often characterises
men who give too much thought to their work to
be able to think too much of themselves kept him
so long at his desk in that shipping office; for when,
after he had contributed many articles to its columns,
he ventured to call on the *Morning Leader* editor on
the chance of getting a regular engagement, there
was no hesitation in finding an opening for one
who had, as an outside contributor, proved his
capacity. From 1904 he was on the staff of the
Leader, and went over to the *Daily News* when the
two papers were amalgamated. In 1914 he was
sent as War Correspondent into France and Belgium,
and in 1915 became one of the official correspon-
dents at the British G.H.Q. out there. He came
home to exchange reporting for the literary editorship of the *Nation*, and resigned that position a
few years ago, having at length established himself
as a writer of books.

The first of his books, " The Sea and the Jungle"
(1912), was the outcome of a voyage up the Amazon
in a tramp steamer carrying a cargo of railway
metals. One of the ship's officers, a relation of his,

had urged him to go, and the *Morning Leader* readily commissioned a series of articles recounting his experiences. It was the sort of journey across the world into unknown places that you may depend he had dreamed of in those Poplar days when he haunted the Docks and, later, when he was cooped in the Leadenhall Street office preoccupied with the dull clerical side of the shipping trade, but the opportunity for such an adventure had not come until now, when he was married and had children and was slightly nearer forty than thirty; and that he did not find it easy to break away from long-settled habits of home and business life you learn from the opening pages of " The Sea and the Jungle ". It came about one morning when he had gone to town by the 8.35 as usual, and was, as usual, sitting in his *Morning Leader* room, "dutifully and busily climbing the revolving wheel like the squirrel ", that the door suddenly opened, "and there was the Skipper smiling at me ". They went out together, and their talk ended in the Skipper insisting on his accompanying him on that voyage:

"I laughed at him. 'What,' I asked conclusively, 'shall I do about all this?' I waved my arm round Fleet Street, source of all the light I know, giver of my gift of income tax, limit of my perspective. How should I live when withdrawn from the smell of its ink, the urge of its machinery. '*That*,' he said. 'Oh, damn that!'"

316

H. M. TOMLINSON

And though " it is a mockery to captives like ourselves to pretend bondage is puffed away in that airy manner ", the newspaper acquiescing in it, the escape became possible:

"Indeed, with this and that, I found the initial step in the pursuit of the sunset red a heavy load, and hardly suited to the constitution of men who have worked into a deep rut; but that high resolution and a faith equal to belief in the liquefaction of the blood of St. Januarius are needed to drop the protective routine of years, to sheer off the dear and warm entanglements of home and friendships; to shut the front door one bleak winter evening when the house smells comfortable and secure, and the light on the hearth is ironic in its bright revelation of years of ease and stability till then not fully appraised; and so depart in the dusk for an unknown Welsh coaling port, there to board a tramp steamer for a voyage that has some serious doubts about it, though its landfall shall be near the line, and have palms in it. The door slammed, I noticed, in a chill and penetrating minor, an incident of travel I have never seen recorded. Now do I come at last, O Liberty, my loved and secret divinity! Your passionate pilgrim is here, late, though still young and eager eyed; yet with his coat collar upturned for the present. Allons! the Open Road is before him. But how the broad and empty prospects of his freedom shudder with the dire sounds and cries of the milk-churns on Paddington Station!"

The narrative of that voyage from Swansea to the Brazils, thence for two thousand miles along the forests of the Amazon and Madeira rivers, on to Barbados and, by way of Jamaica, to Florida, and so home is one of the freshest and most brilliant

317

stories of travel in modern literature. The journey
ended in 1910, and the book appeared two years
later. By 1913 it reached a second impression, by
1920 a third, by 1925 a fourth, and in 1927 it was
issued in a new edition. Meanwhile, Tomlinson
had, in 1919, collected some of his miscellaneous
sketches in "Old Junk", and in 1921 published his
reminiscent and imaginatively descriptive, intimately
realistic studies of "London River".

The shadow of the war is all over "Waiting for
Daylight" (1922). He saw enough of its barbarities
at the front, of the price of victory as it was paid
by the men on the field and by the people, especially by the poorer people, at home, and writes here
with a wisdom born of experience, an infinite pity
that comes of a knowledge of such things. He is
whimsical, ironic, sometimes a little bitter in dealing
with the doings of politicians, important and other
persons who prosper and get riches and honour out
of the general martyrdom, and his sympathies here,
as in all his books, are with the "nobodies", the
"simple souls", the common people who, as he says
in "Old Junk", are always left to do "the hard and
dirty work", and make the world "habitable again,
though not for themselves".

"Tidemarks", in 1924, is the story of another
voyage, a series of vivid sketches of things seen and
heard and done and thought on a journey to Malaya.

318

H. M. TOMLINSON

If I had space there are many passages I would like
to quote: bits of sinister or lovely pictorial beauty,
swift little character studies, humorous or dramatic
incidents, or passing reflections such as that on "how
faithful and bounteous, a spring of original life is
common humanity everywhere!" which brings him
to a war-time recollection:

> "I don't know what the positive evidence for immortality
> may be. I have never seen it. I don't know how it can
> be proved that we are the sons and daughters of God. But
> when I remember the sergeant who called to his men toiling
> through the mud and wire where the shells were falling,
> 'Come on you, do you want to live for ever?' and when
> I recall, as I must when most fearful for the meek at heart,
> the smiling forbearance of another man when he looked at
> the error and hate that were to extinguish his good will,
> then I think there must be a light that can never go out."

Further collections of his newspaper articles,
"Under the Red Ensign" and "Gifts of Fortune",
both published in 1926, were followed in 1927 by
his first novel, "Gallion's Reach", which gave him
rank at once among the ablest, more finely artistic
as well as most successful of contemporary novelists.
He has not drawn himself in its chief character,
James Colet, but it is largely autobiographical, in
that so much of its detail is compounded of his
memories of the Leadenhall Street shipping office,
of Poplar, of his sea voyages and his wanderings in
strange tropical countries, and it gives full scope

319

to the descriptive and story-telling gifts that lend such power and charm to his chronicles of travel. Eight books in sixteen years is not a remarkable quantity, as books are written nowadays, but then Tomlinson's books count also as literature, and you cannot say that of many that are written now.

MARY WEBB

It has often been said—I used to say it myself, before I changed my mind—that much good work in literature is completely overlooked; that authors, neglected in their lifetime, die and are forgotten, and their books, that are as worthy of remembrance as are many that are fully remembered, pass out of knowledge when the few who found delight in them have passed out of life. The suggestion is that if a book fails to take a sure hold on the public while its author still survives, there is very little likelihood of its doing so afterwards, and that in this way, because they have failed to attract our attention in time, many good books have been lost to us.

All I can say is that, dredging in old book shops and ranging over booksellers' catalogues and occasionally through those in the British Museum Library, I have kept a look out for some of these lost ones and have never found any. I have found plenty that were competent and readable; some that have had distinctive qualities; but none that has been good enough to be called great, none that has, on the whole, been better than third or fourth rate. What is truer is that even the greatest author, whose greatness is loudly acknowledged in his day, falls steadily from his high estate in the ten or maybe twenty years immediately following his death; then he begins to revive, his value is reassessed, and by common consent he is carried back, possibly to the place from which he came or even to a height above that, but probably to a more or less lower level where he will settle into his permanent niche. I remember, at the funeral service of B. W. Matz, hearing Sir Hall Caine propound this as the usual order of things in the world of letters, and declare that if this revival does not come about within twenty years or so at most it may never happen, and a writer of genius, though he escape extinction, may linger on, appreciated by the few, but never rising out of that twilight into the fame that is his due. He went on to say that Dickens narrowly escaped from drifting into this condition.

I have doubts of that, for I have reached a conviction that all books of any greatness have absorbed the spirit and vitality of their authors, are alive with a vigorous life of their own and cannot so easily be extinguished. Over and over again books of some greatness have seemed to sink into a moribund state; they have been scarcely read or talked of for a few years, for two or three decades; then, almost as if by their own volition, they have begun to make themselves known again, to force themselves into notice, critics who might have discovered them sooner, but did not, have rallied to their assistance, roused the public to admire them, and enthusiastically crowned with glory authors who could win none so long as they were working for it.

That was how things went with Mary Webb and her work. She was born about 1881, at Leighton, Cressage, Shropshire, where her father, George Edward Meredith, was a schoolmaster. All her early life was passed in Shropshire and elsewhere along the Welsh border among the scenes and people she has re-created with such graphic and intimate realism in her novels. In those early years her family was not in affluent circumstances, and I have heard that when she started writing and needed paper and stamps and occasional books and magazines, to make a little money for herself she grew roses in her father's garden and stood in Shrewsbury market to sell them. She married H. B. L. Webb, a schoolmaster, in 1912, and presently came to London and made her home at Hampstead, but was never happier, I think, than when she could escape from town and settle to work quietly in a cottage she had in Shropshire.

Her first novel, "The Golden Arrow", was published in 1916; her second and third, "The Spring of Joy" and "Gone to Earth", in 1917; and like

so many good books published during the Great
War, though they were well enough received by
many critics, they were engulfed and soon lost
in the more momentous distractions of that in-
auspicious period. "The House in Dormer Forest"
followed in 1920, "Seven for a Secret" in 1923, and
her last and best, "Precious Bane", in 1924.

In all these novels she shows an at times almost
uncanny understanding of human character, an
intense love of nature, a subtle art and imaginative
power in picturing a scene, in the telling of a story,
and a feeling for the magic of words, a beauty of
style that none of her contemporaries surpassed.
Such work as hers could not fail of appreciation by
discriminating readers, but the reviewers gave her
no special attention; they generally acknowledged
that her books were very good but were not
enthusiastic, and, except for the last of them, their
sales were not large—they had the few months of
struggling existence that is the lot of most novels,
and then went out of print. There may have been
others, but I know of only one reviewer who showed
greater critical insight and promptly realised the
something of greatness that is in those novels of
Mary Webb's. This was Edwin Pugh. His was
at that time very much of a voice crying in the
wilderness, and I remember how courageously and
persistently he proclaimed her genius in reviews for

the *Bookman* of her fourth and fifth novels, in a long and glowingly appreciative article on her and her work in general, and in a review of her last novel, "Precious Bane", of which he wrote:

"She has a style of exquisite beauty which yet has both force and restraint, simplicity and subtlety; she has fancy and wit, delicious humour, and pathos of the finest and most delicate, almost subliminal gifts of characterisation and visualisation—she sees and knows men aright, as no other English woman novelist does; she can, moreover, tell a story and so intrigue you with its sense of inevitableness that it seems more real than reality. She has, in short, genius."

That was in 1924, and one took it as a sort of confirmation of Pugh's judgment when the Femina Vie Heureuse Prize was awarded to Mary Webb for that novel in 1926. I was present when she received this award; her husband and her brother, newly returned from India, had come with her —half her happiness was in having them there to share it with her; and her undisguised pride and delight in the occasion were unalloyed, I am sure, by any thought of how much good work she had had to do before this honour fell to her.

In appearance, she was a small, fragile person, with large, anxious eyes. Her manner fluctuated between shyness and a sort of hesitant self-confidence; she was very highly-strung, worried terribly

about trifles, and so sensitive that she was often
deeply wounded by wholly imaginary slights, and
would come and complain to you of these with a
childishly desperate seriousness at which it was at
times impossible to refrain from laughing, and as
soon as you began to laugh she would see the
absurdity of her agitation over such a trifle and
laugh at herself, and the trouble was over. She was
always in delicate health, and so much dependent
on her moods that sometimes for weeks together
she could not write a line. She did a good deal of
reviewing, was an acute and discerning critic, and
wrote her reviews with all the care and grace of
fancy and beauty of phrase she put into her novels.

Shortly after the appearance of "Precious Bane"
she started to write a new novel which she was
calling "Armour Wherein He Trusted". It looked
as if she were now about to come into her own.
"Precious Bane" sold steadily, and went into a third
edition, and continued selling, and a publisher
readily signed an agreement giving her liberal terms
for her new novel before he had seen any of it. But
failing health and her difficult moods retarded its
progress; a nervous breakdown left her neurotic
and subject to fits of deep depression; and in two
years she had barely half of the new book done. A
few days after she told me this, she called me on
the telephone in evident distress, began saying how

unwell she had been, then interrupted herself to say abruptly, "I have destroyed all I had done of the new novel." There was no immediate reply to my surprised, "Good lord, whatever made you do that?" and I have seldom heard anything more piteous than the subdued, broken sound of her crying at the other end of the line. Presently, when she could speak again, she blamed herself miserably, said she had felt so dissatisfied, felt she could not finish it, and would never write any more, so, on a sudden impulse, had torn it and put it on the fire. By degrees she quieted down, and before we finished talking was reconciled to making the best of things, said she could recall it all almost word for word and would set to at once and rewrite it. But within two months she was dead, and that novel remains a fragment.

Her death in October, 1927, attracted very little attention. It was referred to in three weekly journals and in one monthly magazine; it looked as if she were on the way to be forgotten; and no more was said of her anywhere until April, 1928. Then, at a Royal Literary Fund Dinner, the Prime Minister, Mr. Baldwin, referred to her as a writer whose genius had been strangely unrecognised. He had read one of her books, he said, a year before and being greatly struck by it, mentioned Mary Webb to Sir James Barrie and John Buchan, and they told him "she is about one of the best living writers and no one buys her books." She died recently, he added, and "no notice of any kind was paid to her in the newspapers." However that may have been, notice enough was paid to her in the newspapers next morning; they not only reported the Prime Minister's speech but broke out into glorious eulogies of the novelist he had named, crowning her, in lavish headlines, "Wonderful Mary Webb," and "A Neglected Genius." Some were so uncertain about her that they said she had had to support an invalid husband, which was a flight of imagination; and some, giving a list of her novels from "Who's Who", included that "Armour Wherein He Trusted" which she had destroyed in manuscript, with the result that the public went asking for that book at bookshops and libraries in vain, and asking in vain for most of her others, for they were all out of print, except "The Golden Arrow" and "Precious Bane", both of which, the latter because it had been so successful, had some while before been re-issued in cheap editions.

It seemed a lamentably ironical thing that the reading public, having so long and stubbornly ignored the promptings of the literary critics, should immediately accept a politician as their guide in such matters and rush to buy the books of an author he had casually praised in an after-dinner speech.

MARY WEBB

But that is how things happen in this world, and the incongruity would not matter if they only happened in time. But, in this case, they happened at least six months too late, and reading all that generous but belated laudation one had a regretful consciousness that, to apply to herself some lines from "An Old Woman", one of the most poignant of her poems in that volume for which she could find no publisher (but which is now to be included in the collected edition of her works that Jonathan Cape is publishing):

"This would have pleased her once. She does not care
    At all to-night.
They give her tears, affection's frailest flowers,
And fold her close in praise and tenderness.
She does not heed."

REBECCA WEST

REBECCA WEST

THERE is an interesting fragment of autobiography
in Miss Rebecca West's latest book, "The Strange
Necessity". Writing of how a man who goes out
from his own people to live on an alien soil cannot
attain his full intellectual growth, she says she is
"mindful that my father was a member of an English
family settled in the south of Ireland since the reign
of Edward VI, that I am descended from one of
the first governors of Madras, that one of my close
relatives is counted as a maker of British Africa,"
and she adds rather cryptically, "the more I live
in intellectual circles the less does this heredity
displease me."

Her mother was a Scot and father, Charles Fair-
field, was an Englishman, of County Kerry; but
she spent her early years in Edinburgh, where she
went to school at George Watson's Ladies' College,
and you may take it that her memories of Edinburgh
are gathered into that admirable first and best part
of her novel, "The Judge", and that if she did not
go typing in a solicitor's office, like Ellen Melville,
of that story, she is looking through Ellen's eyes

when she describes what Ellen could see from the office window:

"The world, indeed, even so much of it as could be seen from her window was extravagantly beautiful. The office of Mr. Mactavish James, Writer to the Signet, was in one of those decent grey streets that lie high on the northward slope of Edinburgh New Town, and Ellen was looking up the side street that opened just opposite and revealed, menacing as the rattle of spears, the black rock and bastions of the Castle against the white beamless glare of the southern sky. And it was the hour of the clear Edinburgh twilight, that strange time when the world seems to have forgotten the sun though it keeps its colour; it could still be seen that the moss between the cobblestones was a wet bright green, and that a red autumn had been busy with the wind-nipped trees, yet these things were not gay, but cold and remote as brightness might be on the bed of a deep stream, fathoms beneath the visitation of the sun. At this time all the town was ghostly, and she loved it so. She took her mind by the arm and marched it up and down among the sights of Edinburgh, telling it that to be weeping with discontent in such a place was a scandalous turning up of the nose at good mercies."

And if, again, in her Edinburgh days, Rebecca West did not, like Ellen, go out defiantly and sell *Votes for Women* in the streets, it is more than likely that she did so somewhere, for she was an ardent suffragist in those stirring times when women were fighting for their freedom. When she came to write, possibly because she was identified with the idea of women's emancipation and Ibsen was

accepted as one of the prophets of the movement, it was assumed that she had taken her
pseudonym from the Rebecca West of his play,
"Rosmersholm", but she has denied this; she took
the name without any thought of Ibsen and simply
because, in the language of Mrs. Gamp, "she felt
so dispoged".

Before she was twenty, Rebecca West was reviewing books for the *Freewoman*, and writing about
political affairs on the staff of the *Clarion;* she
continued to do these things for the *Daily News*,
the *New Statesman*, and to write on social and miscellaneous topics for other English and American
periodicals; and is doing so still. She is one of
the wittiest and cleverest of living writers; her judg-
ments in literature are as acute as they are confident;
she has the devastating candour of an *enfant terrible*,
but can be as generously enthusiastic in her praise
as she is ruthlessly satirical in her censure, and as
merciless to her friends as to unfortunate strangers.
There is a capital hasty little portrait of her in
Beverley Nichols' "Are They the Same at Home".
It seems Miss West had been told she had "magnetic
eyes", and Nichols remarks, "I suppose she has,
but somehow they are not the features on which
I should have fastened. I should have said, instead, that she had a rather impertinent mouth,
and extremely humorous eyes that pop from side

to side in perpetual amusement at the follies of life.''

But in her serious moods the glancing eyes grow quiet in dreaming, and assume that aloof and more intent expression; and sometimes while you read what she has written you are conscious of those brooding magnetic eyes looking thoughtfully out upon you from what you are reading, and sometimes (frequently) it is the impertinent mouth that laughs at you between the lines, and the extremely humorous eyes that go popping from side to side all down the page. But her impertinences are seldom entirely flippant; there is generally a soundly critical sting in the tail of them, and she has the deftest hand for flashing a simple truth on you the more vividly in an extravagant or whimsical image. As when (in her book on ''Henry James'') she describes Carlyle's style as bewilderingly reminiscent of a railway accident; or says (in ''The Strange Necessity''), ''It is rarely possible to feel liking for Dante, who has that air of taking local politics seriously which makes the Minor Prophets so unlovable'', or, reviewing Mrs. Humphry Ward's Recollections, protests that ''Mrs. Ward, who alone among authors writes as though she were carrying an umbrella in the other hand, reproaches a fellow-writer for lack of charm'', and in face of that popular novelist's superior literary pretensions admits that

334

"there is nothing to be said when a sound and serviceable piece of mahogany furniture insists that it is really Chippendale".

For all its perversities, including an elvish tendency to hand her sitter bouquets with one hand and take them away with the other, Miss West's critical study of "Henry James" (1916) is an extraordinarily able and penetrating analysis of James's method and difficult style and manner of thought. What is finest in James's fastidious, intricate, supersubtle prose is sensitively appreciated, his weaknesses are not spared, for Miss West has no abnormally developed bump of reverence, and the book is an excellent blend of criticism and entertainment; two things that too rarely go together. The academic and the orthodox, who take their literature solemnly instead of seriously, might look askance at this dashing, capable free-lance invading their sanctities and carrying so lightly the knowledge, intuitions and general critical equipment which they wore so much more ceremoniously, but her reputation as a critic of discernment and courage had got on its feet and, with her fugitive newspaper articles, had been well in the running before her first book appeared to justify and increase its progress.

Then, in 1918, with "The Return of the Soldier", she broke out suddenly as a novelist, and proved in this and later in "The Judge" (1922) that she

335

was as able to write stories as to criticise them. "The Return of the Soldier" (which was recently dramatised and successfully produced) is a subtle and poignant study in a post-war psychological problem—the story of a shell-shocked soldier who, suffering from loss of memory, forgets the existence of his wife and remembers only his earlier years and the other girl he had loved before he was married. The means by which his memory is restored to him may be a little of a concession to conventional sentiment, but then conventional sentiment happens to be a real and true thing, and it is not always possible to find an adequate substitute, and the incident is handled with a freshness as well as with a fineness and intensity of emotional power that are not dreamt of in the conventional novelist's philosophy. "The Judge" is planned on larger lines; its characterisation is stronger, richer in life and colour; and if the beauty and normally human qualities of the first part of the book had been carried into the second, instead of lapsing there into bizarre and somewhat squalid tragedy, this might have been the greater story that, from all she has done, we are expecting of her. There have long been rumours that she is engaged on another novel; twice it has figured in her publisher's lists without a title; but we are still waiting for it.

336

And while we are waiting comes "The Strange Necessity", nearly two-thirds of which are occupied by the elaborate essay which gives the book its title, a selection of Rebecca West's shorter miscellaneous essays in criticism being gathered into the remainder. These brief essays have all the quick insight, the piquant humour, impudence, acuteness, the quieter, lucid, studious critical exposition, the generously discriminating praise and the unmerciful hard-hitting qualities we have grown to regard as native to her genius in this art; but, except for occasional bursts of her characteristic whimsicality and irony, the long dissertation on "The Strange Necessity" is overlaid with a solemnity and opaque portentousness that bewilder and disquiet a mortal reader.

The proposition expounded in this treatise, and expounded with a good deal of knowledge and profundity, is that "we have strong grounds for suspecting that art is at least in part a way of collecting information about the universe", and it is supported by a close and at times beautifully suggestive analysis of the symbolism of James Joyce's "Ulysses", and a consideration of how science, in its different fashion, is collecting similar information, the only efforts of science considered, however, being the activities of Professor Pavlov in the dissection of dogs. Surely the artist's methods are more nearly allied to those of the botanist, the geologist, the astronomer. We are asked to admire the skill with which Professor Pavlov removes the brains from his dogs in order to ascertain to what extent their natural instincts will survive that removal; and the wonderful expertness with which he carries out another experiment on the poor beasts and transplants "the opening of the salivary duct from its natural place on the mucous membrane of the mouth to the outside skin, or the cheek or the chin." The animal is loosely strapped on a stand, glass funnels and tubes connected to the displaced duct are carried into another room where an experimenter watches an electric register "that tells the amount of saliva which is secreted". Food is shown to the dog, and (though "this does not happen with a dog whose brain has been removed") saliva flows from the displaced gland. The food is not given to the dog; it is taken away, and when it is shown to him again, a smaller quantity of saliva flows. After the dog has been fooled like this once or twice his expectation is so diminished that at sight of the food no saliva flows at all. Unless his brain has been removed, any man who owns a dog and cares for it sufficiently to note and understand its character, habits, instincts would know, without needing to mangle it and play tricks with its anatomy, that these would be its inevitable

338

reactions in such circumstances, and the experiment is about as futile as it would be to transfer the works of a clock so as to find out whether they will keep going in front of its face as well as behind it. And when Miss West remarks, "these experiments are carried on by a number of people who must have a sort of creative imagination not at all unlike the artists'," I suspect her of dropping into irony and pulling our legs. It is because they are so unimaginative that these experimenters can calmly cut and deform their victims and are quite incapable of realising anything they cannot actually see. The difference between Professor Pavlov and the creative artist is emphasised by Rebecca West herself when, later in the essay, she praises Trollope for the astonishing accuracy with which (probably not knowing how he did it) he psychologised human beings; and this would not have been astonishing at all if he had not been able to do it without unimaginatively cutting them open, to see if they could still carry on business with their brains out and go on loving when their hearts were in the wrong place.

If I believed that Miss West was not writing ironically in what she says of the perfectly obvious results of those barbaric experiments, I should believe one of her reviewers when he wrote the other day that, as a critic, she was not only wonderfully capable, subtle, brilliant, but cruel. She used

339

to be cruel, but she is not so cruel as she used to be. Few of us are. Cruelty is nearly always a normal attribute of youth—in their criticism of books and people Rose Macaulay, Gerald Gould, Beverley Nichols have been no exceptions to this rule—but time and experience bring it home to us that we are as much in need of mercy as are any of our fellows, and that it is easy enough to raise a laugh by being clever and cruel, but infinitely harder and more expert to kill your man with kindness and so deftly that he scarcely feels the wound.

I would sooner this new volume had been filled with such delightfully impertinent, shrewdly revealing essays as those on "Uncle Bennett", "The Tosh Horse", such appreciative and discriminating studies as those of Willa Cather, Tomlinson, Hardy, Sherwood Anderson. That one so witty and wise, a personality so attractive, so alertly interested in life and in literature and so gloriously human should settle down to over-subtle, extravagantly psycho-analytical, ploddingly scientific essays of the "Strange Necessity" type would be a tragedy, and if I thought it could happen I should take to prayer.